HEALING IN THE DESERT

HEALING IN THE DESERT

FINDING YOUR VOICE ON THE JOURNEY FROM BROKENNESS TO FREEDOM

CHRISTINE D'CLARIO

150 YEARS STRONG
DAVID C COOK

HEALING IN THE DESERT
Published by David C Cook
4050 Lee Vance Drive
Colorado Springs, CO 80918 U.S.A.

A Ministry of Cook Media Global

Integrity Music Limited, a Division of David C Cook
Brighton, East Sussex BN1 2RE, England

Library of Congress Control Number 2025948549
ISBN 978-0-8307-9149-1
eISBN 978-0-8307-9150-7

Printed in the United States of America
First Edition 2026

1 2 3 4 5 6 7 8 9 10

120825

TABLE OF CONTENTS

FOREWORD

I had always wanted to snow ski in Colorado, so I joyfully accepted an invitation to join family and friends for a week. The only problem was that I did not know how to ski. But I loved all sports, so I assumed it would be easy to learn.

Our kids picked it up quickly and took off on the blue slopes with their friends. My husband, Nick, navigated the more difficult black runs with his friends, leaving me on the beginner slopes to work out how to simply stay upright.

On the third day, weary of being left alone, I asked Nick to stay with me so we could ski together. At one point I asked him if he was having more fun with me than he would have been having with the guys. Any husband in his right mind would have answered yes. Nick smiled and said, "Chris, if I was with the guys right now, I would be having much more fun." I was stunned at his brutal honesty. Eager to prove him wrong, I turned and started skiing down a very steep hill, uttering the phrase, "Eat my snow, babe."

Well, I knew I was in trouble about twenty seconds later as I did an unplanned aerial somersault. One ski flew off, and then a very loud *pop, pop, pop* reverberated across the mountains. When Nick caught up with me, he had to call ski patrol because I could not move. The proverb reminding us that "*pride goes before a fall*" proved to be true that day.

I had snapped my ACL, torn my meniscus, MCL and fractured my knee. I needed a hamstring graft to reconstruct my ACL. After surgery, the physical therapist outlined my rehabilitation schedule. I will never forget what he said.

"Mrs. Caine, you have quite the recovery process ahead of you. The accident you had was serious and painful, but it was over very quickly. That will not be the case with your recovery process. It will take many months of focused physical therapy for you to fully recover, and it will involve a lot of pain. You have scar tissue that has formed on your knee, and it will need to be broken up so that you can regain full movement again. You can recover completely or partially, quickly or slowly—it is entirely up to you. **The degree to which you are willing to embrace the pain of recovery is the degree to which you will recover**."

Like the truthful words of that physical therapist, this book is a gift. Christine has not sugar-coated the reality of what it will take to walk in the freedom that Jesus died to give you. It is possible to be free, but you must be willing to embrace the pain of recovery along the journey to freedom.

This book is raw, vulnerable, truthful, full of biblical wisdom, and profoundly helpful. As someone who has walked through the pain of past abuse, abandonment, and adoption, I can say with confidence that if you apply the truths contained within these pages, you will find and walk in the freedom Christ offers.

Christine Caine
Bestselling Author
Founder A21 & Propel Women

UNDERSTANDING THE PREMISE OF OUR LIVES

PREFACE

"I struggle with the thought of living tomorrow."

I spoke the words softly and slowly as tears streamed down my face. I sat without moving as my midwife gazed at me through eyes full of empathy and kindness. Gently holding my hands in hers, she sat patiently, listening to me quietly inhale and exhale.

What did I feel now? Relief? Distress? More sadness? The feelings I'd practiced smothering for over two years had rushed right out of me—toppling one right over another from my very own mouth. My inner thoughts had just become an external monologue, and when I'd gotten to my darkest, innermost thought, I hadn't held back.

I made an attempt to look full in her face, but tears blurred my line of vision. I could only catch glimpses of the wise, discerning woman next to me. But even through my tears, her presence was filled with knowing. She was the first and only person in twenty-six months who had asked me the simplest two questions: "How's your heart? What's happening inside you? Tell me." I knew I couldn't mask my answers. I knew if I tried to hide, this highly interceding woman would see right through me.

So I told her everything.

With tears in her eyes, she uttered a quick diagnosis that shook me to the core. "You have a severe case of postpartum depression. I know it well, because I went through exactly the same thing you're going through with the birth of my children. You're not first and won't be the last. And you're not alone." She referred me to a Christian, Spirit-filled therapist and held my hand literally and figuratively until my appointment. That simple act of attention and kindness very well saved my life.

The path that brought me to that moment is the same one that made healing necessary—I just didn't know it yet. To some degree, I was aware that the thoughts and emotions I was experiencing weren't healthy. But even in the midst of my inner turmoil, it never occurred to me that I *could* do anything about it—let alone acknowledge that I *needed* to.

Me? A Christian? Heal? I'd been there and done that. Or so I thought.

I hadn't been compelled to begin a journey of healing for a number of reasons. For starters, I was depleted. At the time, asking me to begin a healing journey seemed impossible. You might as well have asked me to climb Mount Everest. I was tired and exhausted all the time, and I had resorted to trying to make it through the day. The last thing I was looking for was a journey anywhere.

Yet I felt such shame *because* I was depleted. I knew God's grace. I had experienced His promises being fulfilled in my life.[1] I had been a Christian worship leader for years because I genuinely desired to glorify God. The idea that I, as a believer, could be depressed just didn't make sense to me. I couldn't reconcile depression with belief, and shame kept me a prisoner in silence—but screamed at me every day.

I believe my midwife's questions saved my life. Without her guidance, I don't know that I ever would have known just how serious my situation was. I had already done what I thought was fairly extensive inner healing. But mental health? *That's not for me*, I thought. *I'm ok, I don't need to sit with my thoughts and feelings.*

1. Every name or pronoun referring to God, Jesus, and the Holy Spirit is capitalized as an act of literary exaltation to Him—including those from all Bible translations. On the contrary the word satan (which simply means "accuser") or any other word referring to him is lowercased. He does not deserve honor, and it will never be given on any of my platforms, including this book.

Maybe you're having those same thoughts. *I'm ok, I'm good.* But perhaps behind those thoughts, you're curious. Maybe you have questions. Maybe you're even wondering if you were meant to be reading these words—just as I was meant to be asked my midwife's questions.

Regardless of where you are in life, what season you are in, or precisely how healed you are, these words *are* written for you. No matter who you are, you will see yourself reflected in some part.

In these pages, I share the story of the healing journey that I didn't think I needed. My hope is that by offering insight into my journey, you will be encouraged to begin your own healing journey. This book stands as a testimony to the ability to heal by the very fact that it exists, and it has been carefully crafted as a resource for everyone in need of healing—which is all of us.

INTRODUCTION

My first book, *Prodigal Heart*, was published in 2017. It's centered on the hardships I endured in my childhood up through my early adult life. I detailed some of the consequences that came from those hardships—many of which were brought on through no fault of my own while others were, admittedly, self-induced. But it is a book about overcoming and surrendering. I had lived believing the wounds created from grief, abuse, instability, and pain were too deep to be healed, but God showed me otherwise. Surrendering to the Lord had completely changed my story into one of redemption. With God's grace, I had become living proof that any life can be saved, which is why I shared the details of my redemption—to give hope. Little did I know, that story's end would be the beginning of my most difficult story to date.

I waited to write the dedication until I had finished the manuscript. In its final line, I dedicated the book to my unborn children. I had always wanted to have children, but by this time, I felt that I had arrived at a point where I was prepared to be a mother. The redemptive part of my story had led me to the man who had become my husband. Carlos Caban and I had been in ministry together since we got engaged, and we were a decade into a strong, steady marriage. I had come to understand what being a child of God truly meant, and I was eager to raise children—to nurture them in a healthy and safe home, foster in them a desire to obey and depend on God, lead them with bold faith, and witness who they would become as God created them to be.

Devastatingly, a month after I submitted the manuscript to my publisher, I was diagnosed with infertility. Infertility is a full-blown diagnosis, not merely a symptom of another issue. But it can be caused by other medical issues, as was the case with me. After numerous blood tests, extensive medical exams, invasive imaging, and intensive evaluations, I found out that the same chronic endometriosis that had caused me debilitating pain for years was also at fault for my inability to conceive. My medical reports showed that endometriosis had created so much scar tissue that my womb was basically rendered dead.

I held fast to that first part of my story, to all that I had learned about God and about myself through my spiritual experience of redemption. It was why I was even in a place of longing for children. I had carried and clung to all my hopes and dreams, but with the infertility diagnosis, they blew into pieces. As Carlos and I continued through what became a two-year journey of procedures, treatments, and diagnoses, infertility thwarted us from beginning a family together. My dreams seemed to slowly slip away and my hope with them—until I had neither.

Prior to my infertility diagnosis, I had believed the opportunity to have children would come about, but I also knew it wasn't happening as quickly as I'd expected. With my diagnosis, however, came a new reality: having children might never happen. To say this was a heartbreaking reality does not properly describe this period of mine and Carlos' life together. We desired to lovingly grow our family, but we were left sorrowful, devastated, and hopeless.

A particular verse in the Psalms cuts to the matter of desires of the heart, though it is commonly taken out of context. "Take delight in the Lord, and He will give you the desires of your heart" (37:4) is often misunderstood to mean that God will give you whatever you want, positioning God in the role of a magical genie. When it's considered in the context it appears, however, the verse takes on a very different meaning.

The whole of Psalm 37 describes the ways of the wicked in contrast to the ways of the righteous. It says to commit your ways to the Lord (v. 5) and wait patiently for Him (v. 7). God not only takes care of those who are faithful (vv. 17-18), but He also remains alongside the faithful (vv. 25, 28). The chapter indicates God will not necessarily create a perfectly smooth and easy-to-traverse path, but He will help you navigate it (vv. 23-24).

This verse is instructional. We are directed to "delight in the Lord," which means to find joy in who God is, not what He can give you. It's also informative, explaining a causal relationship. As God becomes your sole focus and you consistently turn your attention to Him, you naturally grow to want what He wants. When your desires organically take shape around His character and your purpose in Him, He gives "you the desires of your heart" because your desires are to do His will, emulate His goodness, and accept His timing. Ultimately, it's about desiring God's plan for your life, regardless of what it is.

My desire to be a mother was pure and of good. I yearned to become a mother and believed children to be a beautiful blessing. I envisioned being a parent as a role that brings deep joy and as a gift God bestows us in this life. But God does not promise to grant us our desires so long as they are pure and good. He promises to give us the desires of our heart when our desires are aligned with Him. We delight in Him first, and we will desire Him foremost.

I slowly came to recognize that in the lead up to my diagnosis, my desire to become a mother had taken the primary position in my heart. I had essentially elevated motherhood to the status of an idol. In a way, it was pulling me away from God because I had begun to want it more than wanting what would draw me closer to Him. My heart was not entirely misaligned with God, but it wasn't entirely aligned with Him either—because I had shifted my desire in front of His, prioritizing my will rather than His.

I knew I was being called to trust God, no matter the outcome. Even if my life was going to turn out vastly different than the way I wanted or hoped, I realized I needed to realign my longing and hope with God's purposes, be them what they would. I knew we don't necessarily lose all other desires when we grow in and focus on intimacy with God, so I did not expect—or really even want—to lose my desire to be a mother. But I knew with a refocused perspective, I would want what would draw me closest to the Lord.

So, I surrendered. I identified the part of myself that was holding motherhood as an idol, and I strove to release it. In my heart and in my prayers, I lay my unborn child at the altar of the Lord. I did not know if I would become a mother, but I did know God promises to take care of the faithful. I resolved myself to "hope in the Lord and keep His way" (Psalm 37:34). My faith in God and my relationship with the Holy Spirit were strong, but I daily sought to remain obedient, focusing on God's will being done in my life. When I could feel despair sinking its claws into me, I anchored myself in the hope I had in the Lord. So Carlos and I spent two years in an arduous process of faith stretching, consistent surrendering, and fervent praying.

After exhausting other options, my doctor advised me to undergo surgery to remove the endometrial tissue. This surgery would potentially restore my womb, though there were various risks and concerns as there are with any surgery. After hearing from medical professionals and praying for guidance, we felt confident to move ahead. We decided to go forward, and the date for the operation was set.

Then, a miracle occurred. Miraculously, God healed me before I underwent surgery in the most remarkable way. During a prayer meeting at church prior to the scheduled surgery, God healed me supernaturally. It was truly a miracle, which my doctor later confirmed when he met with my husband and I post operation. Scratching his head in true confusion, he told us he didn't know how to explain what he'd seen once he'd started the procedure.

"There was nothing there to remove," he began. "It's as though you've been healed—which, by the way, doesn't happen." He was at a loss and had no medical reasoning to provide, but Carlos and I knew exactly what had happened. "This is an actual miracle," he said. He went on, describing my womb to look like that of a teenager's! He confirmed that I was ready to conceive a child, and sure enough, I became pregnant with my son after I recovered, just a few months later.

Becoming pregnant was an answered prayer, one in which I still respond to God with gratitude for His gracious kindness. It is evidence that God does answer prayers, and He is still in the business of miracles. But I share this with both a heart of worship to God and a heart of empathy for others. Not all prayers are answered in this life, or at least in ways we humans can discern, and God's decisions—including how He responds to prayer—aren't always clear to us because His ways and thoughts are higher than ours and beyond our understanding.[2] Yes, I had continued praying to become pregnant while also daily surrendering motherhood.

2. "For my thoughts are not your thoughts, neither are your ways my ways," declares the Lord. As the heavens are higher than the earth, so are my ways higher than your ways and my thoughts than your thoughts" (Isaiah 55:8-9).

I still wanted to be a mother, but I'd repositioned God to the highest place in my life. That time had become a beautiful lesson of surrendering, and I'd drawn even closer to the Lord.

But make no mistake: this was not a case of being rewarded because I learned to surrender. God does not answer prayers based on met expectations or lessons learned. He is not assessment-driven, nor is He achievement-oriented. He does not limit answering prayers to the ones that are prayed perfectly or in just the right way. That type of thinking has absolutely no scriptural backing. But when He answers prayers, we are called to respond in worship and with declarations of the Lord our God. And I will forever praise the Lord for this miracle.

My pregnancy with my firstborn, Ian, was an incredibly smooth nine months. No nausea, no pain, no problems. During my near perfect pregnancy, I was despised by all my fellow mom friends, but that was fine by me. If having such an easy pregnancy meant taking jokes from other moms about being so jealous, I was glad to take them! I was thankful I hadn't had any issues and everything was going so well.

That all changed when I gave birth. Ian's birth was exceptionally traumatic. In short, our lives ended up in grave danger, and we almost didn't make it—both of us. After he was discharged from the most mentally and emotionally torturous days at the hospital's intensive care unit, my approach to dealing with that trauma was by *not* dealing with it. I avoided thinking about what had happened at all costs and simply hoped the nervousness and tension I felt would just disappear, along with the terrifying memories. Of course, they did not just magically go away but, as memories do, crept up on me without warning at any given time. That trauma resurrected itself in full force during my second pregnancy, which came just six months after Ian's birth. Throughout my entire pregnancy carrying my second miracle baby, Kenzi, trauma and all its lingering symptoms hovered at the surface.

Our babies were born just sixteen months apart, which, for the record, was not intentional. Carlos and I like to say that was a kind of heavenly sabotage, and we wouldn't have it any other way. Our children are the actual embodiment of God's grace and mercy. I recognized then and still know now that they are evidence of His promises fulfilled over me. We were—and still are—incredibly grateful for these two little ones.

With my babies arriving into this world, I knew the responsibility God had entrusted to me. Carlos and I wanted to raise our children with Christian principles, biblical values, and a foundational faith. Most of all, we wanted them to grow up loving the Lord. We knew the best way to teach them this would be to model *how* to love the Lord—with our hearts, souls, minds, and strength.

But I slowly came to realize that I was unable to model the biblical outline of how to love the Lord. There I was, a Christian and a worship leader, but I was not equipped for this. I knew enough to recognize that I wasn't functioning at full capacity, but I had yet to make a connection between *functioning* and *loving*. I hadn't put the two together enough to know that in order to love at full capacity, we must be functioning at full capacity. Unconsciously, I thought those were two separate issues. I was far from drawing the conclusion that *healing* is necessary in order to fully love the Lord.

In truth, there is a cost to and discomfort in healing. This is pretty much the case across the board when it comes to healing. Take, for example, someone who experiences a serious knee injury. Physical therapy is often necessary for a full recovery—but it can be tremendously painful. That healing process involves pushing through stiffness, stretching sore spots, and rebuilding weak muscles. The injured knee can feel much worse before it feels better, but the pain and discomfort are necessary to restore function.

The same is true when it comes to us as human beings. In order to function at full capacity, we must heal the parts of ourselves that are hurt. The healing process requires patience, determination, and grit because a healing journey has some painful and tough parts—not for the faint of heart. But make no mistake: *it's worth it.* Our ability to love God and others is dependent upon a constant cycle of healing. The purpose of our lives is to bring glory to the Lord, but if we refuse to acknowledge the need to heal, we cannot fulfill our purpose.

Discovering this realization didn't come easily for me, but as Psalm 37 reminds us, God will not always create a smooth and easy path, but He will be with us as we traverse it. My infertility diagnosis initiated the most difficult healing process I have confronted and undergone to date. But before I could begin healing, I had to come to terms with the fact I needed to heal—a decision that began my journey out of the valley of the shadow of death.

CHAPTER 1

THE PREMISE FOR OUR LIVES: THE SHEMA

"The most important one," answered Jesus, "is this: 'Hear, O Israel: The Lord our God, the Lord is one. Love the Lord your God with all your heart and with all your soul and with all your mind and with all your strength.' The second is this: 'Love your neighbor as yourself.' There is no commandment greater than these." —Mark 12:29-31

With today's GPS technology, we're pretty used to having a clear map for just about anywhere we want to go. And I am certainly a fan of GPS—so much so that I have given mine a name: Gypsy! Running across town for dinner? Check Gypsy. Need the closest grocery store? Search Gypsy. Headed out on a cross-country trip? Plug in Gypsy. But when it comes to navigating life, GPS can't really help us there. The way forward isn't always as clear. We seek fulfillment but sometimes aren't certain how to get there. Add to that seasons of sadness, heartbreaking challenges, and anxiety about the future, and the road can seem shrouded in confusion and doubt.

This is a normal, human response. As both fully God and fully human, Jesus understood this deeply, which is why He provides a clear, concise, and direct roadmap to build meaning and purpose—not once but *three* times in Scripture—yet it often goes overlooked.[3]

3. The roadmap appears in three Gospels: Matthew 22:36-40, Mark 12:28–31, Luke 10:25-28. Though the passage appears in John (13:34-35), its emphasis varies from the other three Gospels.

The most complete version of the roadmap appears in Mark, after Jesus has arrived in Jerusalem with His twelve disciples. Their first stop is the temple courts, where the Sadducees ask Jesus a question while he's teaching, intending to trick Him into contradicting Scripture. But their plan backfires when a scribe overhears their "debate" and notices Jesus gives them a "good" answer. (Scripture's words—not mine.) This teacher would have been a top-tier expert in the Jewish faith, but he recognized knowledge when he heard it—and seized an opportunity when he saw it. So, the scribe looks to Jesus and asks, "Of all the commandments, which is the most important?" (12:28).

We don't get much context around this question. Where was this teacher's head at? Was the man looking to narrow down the commandments so he could focus all his efforts on one? Was he trying to prioritize what he should be teaching? Was he overwhelmed? Confused? Worried? Scripture doesn't indicate that he was ill-intentioned, like the Sadducees who were trying to trap Jesus.[4] Perhaps he was just genuinely curious. Whatever the reason, we know the premise of our lives because he took the chance to ask this question.

The answer Jesus gives is premise-based—meaning, it provides foundational truths upon which we can build our identity and purpose. Jesus tells the teacher, "Love the Lord your God

---

4. The title "teacher of the law" and "scribe" are interchangeable in meaning. The scribes (many of whom aligned with the Pharisees) were, as Matthew Henry puts it, "enemies to the Sadducees." You might think that when Jesus debates so well against the Sadducees, the scribes would have jumped in with support—but they were *all* wary of Jesus. Apparently, only one scribe "had so much civility in him" to make a move and "own that [Jesus] answered well." At first, the comparable passage in Matthew may seem contradictory. Mark says the scribe notices "Jesus had given them a good answer" (v. 28); Matthew says, "One of them, an expert in the law, tested Him with this question." But biblical commentators generally agree that unlike the Sadducees, the scribe wasn't trying to trick Jesus. David Brown, for example, explains that the scribe was likely prideful of his knowledge and had not come to believe in Jesus, but confirms that he asked "an honest-hearted, fair" question, "manifestly in no bad spirit." For more, see "Commentary on Mark 12 by Matthew Henry" and "Commentary on Mark 12 by Jamieson, Fausset & Brown" (*Blue Letter Bible*, BLB, 2025).

with all your *heart* and with all your *soul* and with all your *mind* and with all your *strength*." Then, He gives a second: "Love your neighbor as yourself." He concludes, saying, "There is no commandment greater than these." Jesus tells us exactly what our whole life should be founded upon.

To unpack these verses, most readers would begin with the first and move to the second. I take a less common approach when reading this passage, similar to the way my mind approaches reading in general. I am dyslexic, which is a form of neurodivergency. "Neurodivergency" is just a fancy word that describes when someone's brain functions differently from the norm, which is true for how mine processes information. Science may have their name for it, but I like to think of my brain as more of a "neurokaleidoscope." And my family and team can attest to the constant flow of new and various things that come out of my mind. I'm usually thinking and processing differently than everyone else.

With dyslexia, I naturally tend to process text backwards. When I was in grade school, I wrote in my notebooks starting from the last page and moving backwards. It was comfortable for my brain, like the kind of comfort you feel when you get home after a crazy day, take off your shoes and work clothes, and get into something comfy and loose. It's how my brain could "breathe." Then, a teacher who graded the tidiness of our notebooks forced me to write front to back, in the standard way. I learned that to be in the real world, I sometimes had to bend my neurodivergence to fit in, and in this case, avoid sacrificing a good grade. But I still find comfort the unconventional back-to-front way. Whereas most people take a forward-facing perspective, reading left to right, I feel more comfortable doing the reverse—which is actually how I came to understand this passage. When I viewed it backwards, not only did the endgame become clear, but the map to fulfillment did as well.

The map is this: Love yourself *so that* you can love God and love others. To love fully involves your whole being, which consists of four integral parts: heart, soul, mind, and strength. When each part is healthy and healed, your being becomes whole. Only when your being becomes whole can you love with your whole self.

The key is not in just loving, but loving *well.* You must love yourself well, so that you can love others well and love God fully.

And you must *heal* to become *whole.*

The four elements that make up your being must be healthy in and of themselves for two main reasons. One, they function separately to accomplish their individual duties. And two, they come together to form an actual whole. They must be healthy individually first—separate from one another—in order to work as a collaborative unit. If one is not healthy, it won't take long and another will be down for the count as well. But when all four elements are healthy, you are able to function at full capacity—loving with your whole being, giving of your full self. This is very much an all or nothing scenario.

Think about the four legs of a beautifully crafted table built to sustain weight. If any one of the legs is off just slightly, the whole table suffers. If a leg is too long, too short, or too worn, the table won't be balanced or sturdy. Similarly, the table of our life has four legs: the emotional leg, the spiritual leg, the mental leg, and the physical leg. If any one of those is either too long, too short, too tight, or too loose, our life can lose balance or the ability to sustain God's calling on our life. It might even collapse under the pressures of this world. Keeping all four legs in good shape by paying attention to all four is the key to living an abundant life.

When Jesus outlines the premise of our lives in Mark 12, He emphasizes our whole self. With a little digging into Scripture, we can see just how much of an emphasis. Jesus' instruction to "love others as yourself" is less about the humanistic approach of putting yourself first, and more about the true way to love yourself well: loving God. The greatest act of self love is doing the personal work it takes to love the Lord with *all* the heart, soul, mind and strength. The healing, breakthroughs, growth, character, and freedom that comes from this work is the most self-nurturing work we can do for love. And, of course, when a good thing happens to us, we automatically share it. That's loving others as ourselves. It's doing what we can to help and encourage others to thrive in their love of God.

Before I discuss the four elements of self in more detail, let's first walk through some historical context to get a good look at the larger picture.

The Shema

In Mark, Jesus echoes a passage from the Old Testament that His New Testament audience would have known by heart: the Shema. The "Shema," Hebrew for "hear" or "listen," is a declaration of God's oneness and a call to love Him fully. It comes from Deuteronomy, when Moses gives his final instructions to the Israelites before they enter the Promised Land.

Making it to the border of the Promised Land had been a years-long journey for the Israelites. Forty to be exact. Four hundred if you count the years they lived in Egypt.[5] They had progressively become oppressed under Egyptian rule, until their suffering became extremely severe. They cried out to God, and He answered by delivering them out of their captivity in Egypt to the land He had promised their forefather, Abraham, that his descendants would inhabit. But when the Israelites were on the

5. Exodus 12:40-41

verge of entering, they hesitated—and then they panicked. They became so focused on the size of the people who were already living there that they flat out refused to go in. They fed into their fear, and it distorted their perspective.

By this point, the Israelites had seen God's miracles and His power firsthand. He parted the Red Sea so they could walk through it (Exodus 14), used a cloud during the day and fire at night to guide them through the wilderness (Exodus 13), delivered food right out of thin air (Exodus 16), and drew water out of a rock (Exodus 17). But even as close as they'd made it to the Promised Land, their fear overshadowed the miracles they'd seen. Though God forgave them (Numbers 14:20), they wandered in the desert for 40 years before finally entering the land.

Imagine living in an actual desert for forty years, let alone wandering around all over it. I doubt many of us could survive our front yards for too long—myself included. And if you're thinking about a flat desert full of sand dunes, think again. The Sinai Desert, where the Israelites likely spent the majority of the forty years, is made up of rock and filled with dust. The wilderness would have been exceptionally harsh and barren, with very little food and water. That desert gets less than two inches of rain *a year*. Temperatures would have been extreme, with blazing heat during the day plummeting to a chilling cold at night. Those dangers don't even take into account all the creatures slithering, crawling, and sprinting across the desert while they slept in tents and walked in sandals.

And yet, the Israelites survived. However, they did not survive on their own. They learned to rely entirely on God for everything—food, water, protection, and guidance. Their journey was emotionally draining, mentally taxing, physically exhausting, and generally disorienting. They had no long-term plan-of-action set out before them, but they did have day-to-day directions that

God consistently provided. By learning to trust God's guidance as they wandered, they experienced a process that changed them significantly, and they entered the Promised Land as transformed people. The time the Israelites spent in the desert was a formative period that shaped their identity and development as a nation.

Before the Israelites entered their land, Moses wanted to be sure they would remember and honor God's faithfulness. He gathered them together at its border, near the same place their previous generation had refused to enter forty years earlier. Here, Moses said, "Hear, O Israel: The Lord our God, the Lord is one. Love the Lord your God with all your heart and with all your soul and with all your strength." Moses' words became the opening statement of the Shema, a foundational declaration of faith, recited daily in Jewish tradition.

The fact that this Great Commandment came at the end of the Israelites journey through the desert, right before they entered the Promised Land, blows my mind every time I think about it. Moses could have said anything, but God made sure this is what remained in their hearts after such an arduous forty years. Praise the Lord.

The Four Elements of Self

Moses' audience generally viewed the self holistically. Ancient Hebrew culture didn't think of the heart, soul, mind, and body as separate. The mind, specifically, was rolled into the self. The original Hebrew words for "soul" (*nephesh*) and "heart" (*lev*) involved the mind—but in a holistic way.[6] For them, the inner life was centered in the heart as the source of thought, feeling, and will, and in the soul as the living self.

---

6. Brown, Francis, S. R. Driver, and Charles A. Briggs. *The Brown-Driver-Briggs Hebrew and English Lexicon: With an Appendix Containing the Biblical Aramaic.* Hendrickson Publishers, 1996.

By the time Jesus was walking around in the first century, Jewish culture had been heavily influenced by Greek language and thought. Unlike ancient Hebrew culture, Greeks treated the mind as a distinct aspect of the person—in large part because of the philosophical thinkers of their culture. Greek philosophers believed that reason—the human capacity to think clearly and rationally—was central to knowing what is real. They identified the mind as the source of both logic and reason, so they emphasized it as a separate part of the self.

When Jesus recited the Shema, He was speaking to a Jewish religious audience that had been culturally influenced by Greek and Roman thought. Aware of this Greco-Roman influence, He expanded on the Shema, adding "with all your mind." To be sure, He wasn't altering the Shema; He was simply drawing out its full intent. He was making sure His audience understood that they were to love God with their *whole* self—because for them, adding "mind" emphasized the whole person. This is true for our modern Western civilization too. After the fall of the Roman Empire, Western civilization clung to the Greek model, so our modern Western culture still makes these separate distinctions, giving us four elements of self.

It's interesting that Jesus didn't take this moment to make some philosophical argument, proclaiming the old way of thinking was better than the new way, or one right and the other wrong. He simply acknowledged this particular cultural view had shifted and tailored His answer in a way that delivered His point: love God and love people with your *whole* self. His description gives us a clear picture of the premise of our lives and what it truly means to love *well*—beginning with our heart.

Heart, Emotional Being

The heart has long been considered the origin source of emotions. From about 2,000 to 400 BC, the ancient Hebrews believed that feeling deeply was a reflection of the heart's engagement with God, life, and people in general. In the fourth century, the Ancient Greek philosopher Aristotle (384-322 BC) identified the heart as the organ associated with emotions.[7] The meaning of "heart" in the original Greek—*kardias*— means the center or seat of our thoughts and feelings. Fast forward a few centuries to medieval Christian philosopher Thomas Aquinas (1225–1274 AD). He combined Aristotle's philosophy with Christian theology and deemed the heart the direct source of human emotions.[8] In the early part of the nineteenth century, Danish philosopher Søren Kierkegaard (1813–1855) believed the heart to be central to deep emotional honesty.[9] (The list goes on, but you get the point.)

In our day and age, Hollywood may have given us some unhelpful notions about the link between the heart and emotions, but the heart still represents our emotional core. Everyone has, feels, and experiences emotions. What we do with them is a different topic (which we'll discuss in more depth later). For now, I'll say that we shouldn't base our actions solely on emotion, but we should still honor and understand what we feel.

Personally, my heart has never known how to feel lightly. I love deeply, and strong emotions have always been a part of who I am. You may be closely in tune with your emotions, or you may have developed a habit of pushing them aside, burying them deep

7. See Chapter 10 in Book 3 of Aristotle's *On the Parts of Animals* (*A New Critical Edition*, edited by David G. Horrell, Oxford University Press, 2020).

8. Pasnau, Robert. "Thomas Aquinas." *The Stanford Encyclopedia of Philosophy*, edited by Edward N. Zalta & Uri Nodelman, winter 2024, https://plato.stanford.edu/entries/aquinas/. Accessed 7 May 2025.

9. In Part I of his work *Works of Love* (1847), Kierkegaard discusses the heart as a source of emotions. In later works, he explores the concept of the heart in relation to the self, emphasizing the "heart" as critical to one's relationship with God.

inside yourself. But allowing our emotions to pass through our bodies and accept them as part of the human condition is critical to our mental health. Our heart and the emotions that flow from it are a part of us, a part of our whole self.

Soul, Spiritual Being

When the Bible speaks about being human, it is not a mere sum of flesh and bones. In the account of Genesis 2:7, we are reminded that God took dust from the ground and shaped it, but life began the moment He breathed life into his nostrils. That image is powerful: without divine breath, the body is nothing more than inert matter; with this breath, man becomes a living being—complete, able to think, feel, and relate to his Creator.

Throughout Scripture, the term *soul* (Hebrew *nefesh*, Greek *psyché*) is used to speak of being spiritual. It is not an ethereal fragment separate from the body, but the person with thoughts, emotions, and will. That is why the psalmist could cry out: "Bless the Lord, O my soul; let all my being bless His holy name!" (Psalm 103:1). It was not a part of him that worshiped, but his whole inner being.

The *spirit* (Hebrew *ruah*, Greek *pneuma*) points to another dimension—the deepest one, the part that comes directly from God. It is the divine breath that makes communion with the eternal possible. Ecclesiastes 12:7 expresses it simply: when life in this world ends, "the spirit returns to God who gave it." The spirit, then, not only sustains life but opens human beings to transcendence in eternal life and to relationship with their Creator.

However, the soul and the spirit are not separate. Hebrews 4:12 affirms that the Word of God is so sharp that it can divide them, which indicates that they are distinguishable, even though in our experience they appear united. Mary expressed this in her song when she said: "My soul glorifies the Lord, and my spirit rejoices in God my Savior" (Luke 1:46-47). In her words, soul and spirit intertwine in a single act of praise.

Jesus Himself, when quoting the Shema in Mark 12:30, commands us to love God with all our heart, all our soul, all our mind, and all our strength. There, the soul appears as a synonym for life—for the inner being. To love God with all the soul means to give Him one's entire existence—what is visible and invisible, what we think and what we feel.

For this reason, we can say that human beings are body, but also soul and spirit. The body connects us to the earth, but the divine breath makes us spiritual beings, capable of knowing God and living in communion with Him.

Mind, Conscious Being

Much like our souls, we cannot see our minds. Thanks to modern medicine and technological developments, brain scans can show images of our brain patterns and activity—but no distinguishing features of our mind. Even a brain scan can't fully determine whether someone is conscious or not.

Your mind is the defining feature that marks you as a conscious being. Because we have minds, we are able to process thoughts. A plant, for example, can't very well do that, even though it is a living organism. "Conscious" is, after all, how we describe our normal state of life. When you are awake, you are conscious. When you faint, you are briefly unconscious. When you sleep, however, you aren't truly unconscious. Think about the last time you had a dream. Sleep is actually considered a state of partial consciousness because sometimes your mind is still at work.

Since your mind doesn't have a designated space or any physical attributes, we can't directly observe it. To make matters even more complex, only you have true access to your mind—the part of yourself that is aware, that perceives, that notices, that discerns. Merriam-Webster's definition of "mind" as "the conscious mental events and capabilities in an organism" illuminates the mind as the center of conscious awareness.[10] The original word for "mind" in Mark 12 is *dianoias*, which refers to deep thought. Its use refers to the mind as the faculty of understanding and desiring—which implies that our desires stem from our thoughts and emphasizes the depth of the conscious *and* subconscious mind.

As conscious beings, we are capable of making decisions based on intentions; reflecting on our emotions, actions, and decisions; using logic, reason, and imagination; and sharing ideas through different languages. Over the years of our lives, we make memories and develop a sense of identity. It is our mind, part of the self, that makes all this possible.

Strength, Physical Being

The body is the most visible of all four of the elements of the self. It's the vehicle that our hearts, souls, and minds travel around in. We are physical beings, requiring oxygen, food, and water. We can't live in temperatures that are exceptionally cold nor extremely hot. We get sick and hurt, and we need sleep to rest, recover, and repair. Yet for as delicate as our bodies can be, they're shockingly resilient. We can bounce back from an injury, overcome dire illnesses, and even survive uninhabitable conditions.

Our bodies also naturally define our physical strength. We are both limited to and empowered by the body's capabilities. A 100-pound high schooler won't bench press anywhere close to as much as a 230-pound bodybuilder. And a football linebacker

10. "Mind." *Merriam-Webster.com Thesaurus*, Merriam-Webster, https://www.merriam-webster.com/dictionary/mind. Accessed 8 May 2025.

won't run a sub seven-minute mile pace that a marathoner can maintain for over twenty-six miles.

The original Greek word, *ischyos*, profoundly influences our understanding of "strength" in Mark 12. It means strength, power, might, and force—but it also involves the extent of our ability. I see the latter as encouragement, almost a pep-talk of sorts, to challenge us not to conform, but to expand beyond our limits for the love of God and His glory. When we think about our strength in this context, we start considering what strengths we have, where they thrive, and how we can develop our strength and expand our abilities in those areas.

God purposefully and intentionally creates us as individuals, our body being a part of His creation. Your physical being is an integral part of who you are. Certainly, a marathoner devotes significant time and effort to training, and a linebacker puts in reps on the field in practice. But genetics play a role in our physical makeup as well. We are all created as different individuals, and we all possess different physical strengths and weaknesses. Most importantly, you are "fearfully and wonderfully made" (Psalm 139:14), with skills and attributes that God has made unique to you.

The Whole Self

If you're like me, you get stressed from time to time. Perhaps you, like myself, have a tendency to take on a bit more than you should, only to realize too late that you've surpassed your bandwidth and maxed out your capacity. To create more time in your day, you start clearing your schedule of any fun activities—after all, they're unnecessary anyway. To get more work done, you forgo some hours of sleep—after all, you can get by just fine. To save time, you grab fast food instead of meal prepping—after all, food is food. Then, if you're *really* like me, you'll catch a cold. It's fair to say a cold is a blip on the radar of life, but the lead up to it is a perfect illustration of how the four parts of your being function.

In one way, the four elements operate *separately from* each other. When you overcommit, you're stressed mentally. As you devote less time to the enjoyments of life, you naturally don't feel as much gladness in your heart. Without resting deeply, your soul becomes weary. Lacking proper nutrition, your body's immune system weakens. At the same time, they work *collaboratively with* each other. As relatively minor of a physical ailment as a cold is, this one didn't start physically. The mind was affected first, but the body ended up being down for the count.

You may not even notice when your choices are negatively impacting any one part of your being. In the case that you do, you might justify your actions with thoughts like *I just need to get through this season* or *it's not that big of a deal* or *I'm stronger than this*. Before my healing journey, I defaulted to this way of thinking. But what we often fail to recognize is just how severely the other three parts are affected as a consequence. While a bit of a nuisance, a cold is pretty easy to bounce back from. But if we do not attend to each part of our being for an extended period of time, we will face more major, life-altering illnesses that are far more difficult to heal—but that doesn't mean we shouldn't.

Beginning in the Desert

The years that the Israelites spent wandering in the desert was a formative period in their history. They became whole as a nation, relying on God for their survival and learning to love Him fully. Although they did not know it at the time, they were living the story they would tell for years to come after entering the Promised Land.

Though you are likely not wandering in a geographical desert as the Israelites were, you may feel as though you are still wandering in a figurative desert. Descriptions of the Sinai Desert—rock, dust, freezing, blazing, harsh, barren, dangerous, wilderness—may resonate deeply with you. I can assure you that they have with me. Fear of failure, hiding in shame, and dread of judgment created my own personal desert. Feeling severely inadequate, sad, and anxious, especially in the midst of experiencing God's miracles, only deepened my shame. I wasn't in a geographical desert, but I was still very much in a desert. I was not loving God with everything in me because I couldn't—I was broken in every way.

My own healing journey started *from within* the desert.

Take it from me, you must come to terms with the fact that you are in a desert before you can find your way out. You have to take a good, hard look at the parts of yourself that are in need of healing. Each part must be healed individually so your whole self can become healthy. Without a fully healed and whole being, you are hindered in your ability to love God fully. A fractured being cannot give itself wholly, so you must first become whole.

The passage in Mark 12 often goes overlooked as the roadmap to fulfillment, but it clearly outlines the premise of our lives. Perhaps it just takes us looking at it with an unconventional—or neurodivergent—perspective to see it.

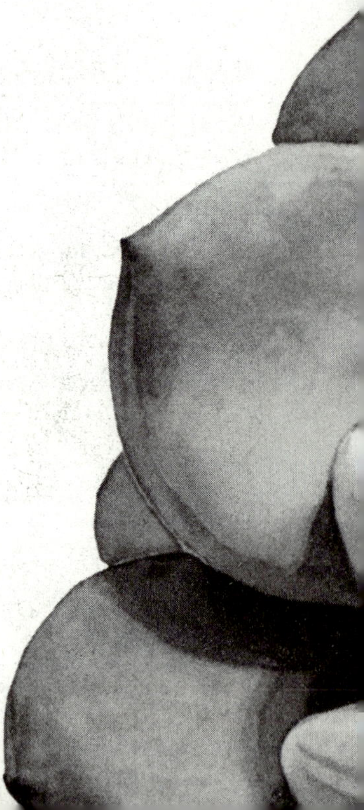

PART I

A VOICE TO DISCOVER —FROM WITHIN THE DESERT

REALIZATION

CHAPTER 2

DISCERNING THE HEALING JOURNEY

I am a Christian leader. I was also suicidal. Let that sink in.

If that is jarring, unsettling, or downright unbelievable, that's understandable. It was for me too, which is why I avoided acknowledging it *and* coming to terms with it. But flat out refusing to avoid a hard truth doesn't make it any less true.

First, I need to explain some backstory—to frame an understanding of the truth.

Practicing Discernment

After my son and I almost died during childbirth, my approach to dealing with that trauma was the same as any other I'd previously experienced: I ignored it. I did everything in my power *not* to think about it. But as unaddressed trauma does, it followed me, and I felt it throughout my second pregnancy. By the time my daughter was born, I was exhausted—in every way, shape, and form. I knew what exhaustion from a newborn was like, but that's not what this was. This was different. The exhaustion was deeper and more intense. It seemed the more I tried to do externally, the more I struggled internally.

For reasons I couldn't pinpoint, I felt like an absolute failure, believing all my efforts in ministry and at parenting were inadequate. *I'm not doing enough, and I can't ever do anything well enough*, I thought. A persistent sense of sadness seemed to loom over me, and I cried all the time. *I don't even know why I'm crying.*

Why am I so sad all the time? I wondered. Then, I felt guilty about being sad. *I shouldn't feel sad because I've been given two beautiful miracles*. I was constantly on edge and tense, never able to catch a break from feeling nervous. Nervousness followed me around everywhere I went, so I couldn't sleep either. *What if something happens to Ian or Kenzi? What if I do something wrong?*

Not only were these thoughts and feelings exhausting, but their causes seemed inexplicable. They didn't make any sense to me. That led me to living in fear of anyone finding out what was going on with me. If I couldn't understand what was going on, how could anyone else? When people came to visit, I often hid in the bathroom so no one could see me. I didn't want to be judged or made to feel any worse than I already did. I managed to muster up every ounce of strength possible to put on a facade in front of my family and friends, just enough to hide the truth. I was trying to survive, day to day, moment to moment.

But appearances were not what they seemed. I was hurting and utterly depleted—heart, mind, soul, and body. My heart felt a deep and unexplained sadness. My mind was working overtime doing mental gymnastics. My soul seemed hard pressed on every side. And my body? It just felt beaten up in general. Physically, my body chemistry was irregular, and my hormones were unbalanced. It was a deadly combination.

I was able to keep this charade up until I was kindly confronted by my midwife. I made it to my last appointment, exactly six weeks after my daughter was born. My midwife did all her usual checks and confirmed I was ready to be released from her follow-up care. Overall, she was pleased with my progress. (I mean, I was leading worship and jumping up and down on a stage just two weeks postpartum, like I didn't just push out a nine-pound-two-ounces baby!) But after she finished filling out her little chart—and, I know, moved by the Holy Spirit—she sat down next to me. That's when she asked those two life-altering questions: *How's your heart? What's happening inside you?* I felt like a wave of heat rushed to my shoulders and up my neck, making quite an uncomfortable stop in my face. I couldn't hide anymore. My body was practically pushing the words out of my mouth. When I told her everything, she cried right alongside me.

Up to that point, no one else had asked such searing questions. On the surface, they're relatively normal questions, but underneath, they cut directly to my heart, soul, mind, and body. Her comforting presence had put me at ease, making me feel as though I could divulge my innermost thoughts. Someone finally had given me the greatest gift for confession: permission, space, compassion, and safety. So I did. I confessed it all. And she was the only person in whom I'd confided, the only person who knew what was actually going on with me. I'd devoted a lot of energy to making sure no one knew the behind-the-scenes brokenness. But in a small way, my hidden truth had come to light.

"You have postpartum depression," she said gently, in return to my outpouring of unfiltered thoughts. "And it's severe," she continued. "I know because I went through it with my children." She paused, her gaze shifting to one of seriousness. "But there is a way out." Reaching into her files, she clasped what I could see was a small card. She handed it to me and explained it was the business card of a therapist she recommends.

"She handles postpartum depression, trauma, all of it," she said. After we talked a while longer, she returned to the subject of the therapist. She was adamant that I call her to set up an appointment. Yet I didn't feel assertive pressure from her. Whether it was her words or the way in which she spoke them, I felt a slight sense of comfort, the first I'd felt in months. It was a smidge of a sensation that I'd almost forgotten.

"I will be calling and texting you every hour until you tell me that you have an appointment with her," she promised before leaving the room that day.

Prior to this conversation with my midwife, I would have never considered going to a therapist. As utterly depleted as I'd become, it never occurred to me that I needed any kind of formal in-office appointment for my mental health. *That's not for me. I'm ok, I don't need to sit with any parts of my life*. Quite frankly, I thought therapy was for other people—not me. I was supposed to be stronger, to press on harder. Yet try as I had to press on, I knew I hadn't gotten far.

I'm not sure what would have happened had she not asked those two wise and discerning questions. For over two years, my midwife had proven herself worthy of my trust. As an intelligent and skilled midwife, she had helped bring my two children into this world. Now, with great wisdom, she had discerned that I was in need of help. The dictionary definition of "discern" is "to perceive or recognize something clearly, often with difficulty or through careful observation." My midwife saw right through the front I was putting on and recognized that I was struggling. Discernment also means having the ability "to distinguish or differentiate between things with clarity or insight."[11] She'd known this was not a case of momentary sadness. With near prophetic insight, she'd leaned into what she was perceiving.

Once my midwife brought her observations to light, I couldn't very well shroud them back into darkness. She had made a clear

11. Discern." *Merriam-Webster.com Thesaurus*, Merriam-Webster, https://www.merriam-webster.com/dictionary/mind. Accessed 10 June 2025.

diagnosis, and I couldn't unhear what she'd said to me. I'd definitely heard her, plain as day. With knowledge from her medical practice and wisdom from her own personal experience, she had outright named what I was facing: postpartum depression. There was some relief in that—in naming what I was going through and knowing I was not alone. But it also brought the truth to light, which was simultaneously disconcerting. She'd diagnosed me with depression. I had a mental illness.

On the one hand, I was hesitant. On the other hand, I'd been presented with the truth of my situation.

Now, it was my turn to practice discernment.

Past History, Present Decisions

Suicidal thoughts are a symptom of depression, which I learned once I got into therapy. This isn't the case for everyone, but it was the case for me. In the months after my second child was born, I began to struggle with the actual thought of living tomorrow. It wasn't that I was not suicidal one day and suddenly suicidal the next. I can't pinpoint exactly when those thoughts started to creep in, but that's what they did: creep. Then, they escalated. I seemed to have reached a point where I just couldn't make sense of life anymore.

This wasn't the first time I'd had suicidal thoughts. I'd experienced that years before. But since then, I'd dedicated my life to the Lord, done what I thought to be extensive inner healing, and seen God perform real miracles in my life. I genuinely believed that being suicidal was in my past, something I'd healed from and overcame. That made being suicidal again all the more excruciatingly painful and disorienting.

The death of my father when I was a child had been the traumatic pivot that spearheaded many traumatic events to follow. He had many addictive tendencies, and he passed away from complications due to alcoholism and drug abuse when I was six years old.

The following year, my mom moved my sister and I from New York to the Island of Puerto Rico. By this time, she was remarried and had given birth to my baby brother. My stepfather was a native "Boricua" (Puerto Rican), who decided to take us out of the city where crime was on the rise and into a safe haven in the tropics. We settled in the rural parts of the northwest of Puerto Rico. Its beauty and year round summer weather was new to me, as was the culture, the language, and the people.

As beautiful as the island was, it quickly became true to me that, though this would be my new home, I wasn't at home in my heart anymore. And I wouldn't be for years to come. Then, I went from being a kid who was bullied for having a tooth deformity, fair skin, green eyes, and afro-Caribbean hair to being a young woman who was labeled exotic and received lots of male attention. In some seriously unhealthy ways, I let one of those guys fill the empty spaces that had opened up in me over the years. When that relationship broke, I broke with it.

Afterwards, I'd tried to straddle a line of living right and wrong for a couple years—leading worship at my church while leading a life the absolute opposite as that of a child of God. That double life had pummeled me all the way to rock bottom, where I'd become depressed and suicidal. I gave God a last minute request, which sounded more like an ultimatum—an "if you're there" kind of thing. I wish I could go back and be more respectful, but God was so kind to look past my tone and see my heart. He made Himself known to me, and I hadn't looked back since.

What I didn't know was that the trauma during my childhood and young adult life was fertile ground for the making of a mental health disorder. With my early life as its origin point, my mental illness had developed over time. Unbenounced to me, I had a history of a mental health disorder that had gone unacknowledged—until it was almost too late.

But there is a way out. My midwife's words reverberated in my mind. I knew that a decision lay before me.

In August 1915, *The Atlantic Monthly* published "The Road Not Taken" by Robert Frost. It later became one of his most famous poems, appearing in textbooks and anthologies all over the country. But at the time, Frost wasn't necessarily well-received by critics. Most of the people who praised his poetry were people who typically didn't like poetry at all. Initially, his audience was drawn to his poetry for its singsong-like rhythms and rhyme schemes. But they remained loyal readers for what he wrote underneath the frolicking verses. With a directness in his words, he cuts to the human condition and describes what it feels like to be alive.

In "The Road Not Taken," the narrator stands in the woods before two paths. He looks at them, assesses both, and ponders which one to take for a long time. This isn't a decision like one you make in the grocery store or out on a Friday night for dinner. He's making a choice that will affect the rest of his life. He knows that the path he chooses will lead to another path, and that one on still to another. In the last stanza, the narrator foretells that he'll look back on his life and know his choice in this moment changed everything. He understands the weight of the choice between the two paths.

Like Frost's narrator, I found myself before two paths. One

path was that of least resistance. At the time, remaining unwell—or worse—seemed far easier. I could just let things ride and succumb to my illness. The other path was that of life, assuredly the more arduous of the two. Outstretched before me was a choice.

Frost's narrator chooses the path "less traveled by," believing he will look back "somewhere ages and ages hence" and see that taking the road less traveled by "made all the difference."[12] Like him, I decided to take the path that wasn't going to be easy. I chose the second path, the path of life, even though I was unsure what life even was beyond mere existence. My hope was that I would look back to see that taking the harder path was well worth the difficulty—and made all the difference.

Healing From Bondage

"Hear, O Israel: The Lord our God, the Lord is one. Love the Lord your God with all your heart and with all your soul and with all your strength" (Deuteronomy 6:4-5) When Moses spoke these words, he was a mouthpiece for God. Delivering God's words to the Israelites, he did so as a leader with authority. But things didn't start out that way for Moses.

Forty years prior, God had dictated to Moses precisely what he should say to the leaders of the Egyptians and the elders of the Israelites when he got to Egypt. One of Moses's concerns was his speaking abilities, which he expressed this concern to the Lord, saying, "Pardon your servant, Lord. I have never been eloquent, neither in the past nor since you have spoken to you servant. I am slow of speech and tongue" (Exodus 4:10). God knew this, of

12. Frost, Robert "The Road Not Taken,". *The Poetry of Robert Frost*, edited by Edward Connery Lathem, 105-106. Penguin Classics, 2002.

course, and He replied to Moses, "Who gave human beings their mouths? … Is it not I, the Lord? Now go; I will help you speak and will teach you what to say" (vv. 11-12). God wasn't going to allow Moses's speech to be a hindrance to the role God needed him for. Quite the contrary. God was going to *use* his voice.

Moses was not only going to have to discover his voice in order to fulfill God's calling, he was going to have to believe in his ability to use it. More than that, he had to believe that God would *give* him the ability. He didn't know it when he was standing before the burning bush, but Moses would go on to speak in front of all kinds of people during his leadership: repeatedly to Pharaoh and his officials (Exodus 5-12), Israelite elders (Exodus 3:16; 4:29), Israelite priests (Leviticus), future Israelite leaders (Deuteronomy 31), and the Israelites themselves. With God's help, he developed his voice as a leader. He'd come a long, long way by the time he spoke the Shema.

Similarly, the Israelites did not know when they left Egypt that they were beginning a story they would tell for generations. As they trekked across the desert, they were focused on the journey before them, and they looked forward to the new season of life they were journeying toward. By the time they reached Canaan, they'd witnessed God perform great miracles all along their trek. Then, they stood at the border, viewing the land of a new life that awaited them.

Metaphorically speaking, I could resonate with this at the point I was diagnosed with depression. Much like the Israelites, I'd made it to the border of a new season as well. Just as God saved the Israelites from captivity and delivered them from Egypt, He had saved me with Jesus. I had moved on from my early life (and its trauma) and was eagerly anticipating beginning my life as a mother. I'd experienced God's miracles along the way, and I stood at the border of a beautiful life before me: a loving husband, a growing family, and a great God at the center.

Becoming suicidal again was incredibly disorienting. I truly believed I had left my early life's trauma in my past. I had certainly wanted to leave it there. Albeit uninvited, it had come with me, similar to Egypt and the Israelites. Theoretically, they'd wanted to leave Egypt and had cried out to God to deliver them. But even though they'd left Egypt geographically, their hearts and minds often returned to their old ways of thinking, stuck in fear and slavery. I felt similar. How could I be having these thoughts after I'd been saved? After I'd experienced God's miracles? After I'd had promises fulfilled over me? I thought I was well past all of that.

The Israelites found themselves back in the same desert from which they'd just come. Much like the Israelites, I felt like I was back where I'd started—this time with what seemed like even more instability and even less certainty. Yet it was the instability and uncertainty of the Israelites' nomadic life that created a deep dependence on God. With no clear destination, they had to rely on His guidance.

From the onset, God made their path clear. Using cloud and fire, He illustrated He was with them: "By day the Lord went ahead of them in a pillar of cloud to guide them on their way and by night in a pillar of fire to give them light, so that they could travel by day or night. Neither the pillar of cloud by day nor the pillar of fire by night left its place in front of the people" (Exodus 13:20-22). When they began their uncertain desert period, God continued guiding them: "From evening till morning the cloud above the tabernacle looked like fire. Whenever the cloud lifted from above the tent, the Israelites set out; wherever the cloud settled, the Israelites encamped. At the Lord's command the Israelites set out, and at His command they encamped" (Numbers 9:15-18).

God never left the Israelites—to wonder *or* wander. *Should we stay or should we go? Which direction should we take? Do we keep straight or turn around?* He left no room for guesswork.

The English word "desert"—first used in 1297—meant "deserving; the becoming worthy of recompense, i.e. of reward or punishment."[13] Viewed alongside the Israelites' story, a desert period becomes an opportunity. Regardless of how we got to our desert, we can either use it to our benefit or allow it to lead to our demise.

When I made the choice to heal, I was in the middle of my desert. By choosing the path of life, I was choosing the healing process. I knew my journey would be difficult and challenging. I began with little direction, and I was unclear where my journey would go. But when I made the decision to begin, I also made the decision to trust God in my suffering. I believed that if I drew near to Him, then He would draw near to me, just as Scripture says. I trusted Him to walk alongside me.

Long before the Israelites desert season, Moses set the example for trusting God. At God's prompting and with His help, Moses found his voice and used it as the leader of the Israelites. His final instructions to the Israelites—recited still to this day—were spoken using the voice God had helped him use for over forty years. The Israelites were able to recite these words and tell their story only after having found their voice as people by trusting God while in the desert.

13. "Desert." *Oxford English Dictionary,* accessed June 1, 2025.

Like the Israelites, the desert became a place where I deepened my dependence on and trust in the Lord. Choosing the more difficult path led me to the point that I am able to tell my own story. The choice I made and the process I persisted through thereafter are the reasons why I am alive today and able to tell the stories you hold in your hands. Though the path wasn't easy, it was not one that I walked alone.

I've learned that the process of healing from past bondage takes time. But having experienced it firsthand, I have also learned of the life-giving nature of a healing journey. That process—my healing, restoration, wholeness—was not only for me. It was also for *you.*

Now, you can receive the wisdom I've accrued thus far—and I call that a win.

CHAPTER 3

DEBUNKING THE MYTH THAT MENTAL ILLNESS ISN'T REAL

Mental illness is real—and it's real for Christians too.

Yet a stigma around mental illness persists in the Church.[14] For whatever reason, Christians have traditionally had a hard time accepting pretty much anything having to do with mental health—certainly mental illness. The Church has no problem with Western medicine or medical physicians. You would never hesitate to mention to someone at church on a Sunday morning that you went to a doctor because you weren't feeling well. You wouldn't tiptoe around saying that you were diagnosed with a sinus infection. But to say you went to a therapist or counselor? Mention that you were diagnosed with depression? Now that's a different story.

This isn't the case for everyone, but in my experience, mental health was a taboo subject in my church upbringing. At the time I was diagnosed with a mental disorder, I was both a Christian and a worship leader. I was also completely oblivious to the fact that I was in dire need of help. I'd been taught some serious misconceptions about mental illness, which had only been reinforced by the Church. I'd certainly never heard of good mental health practices, warning indicators to be on the lookout for, or any related notion about healing the mind.

But as I mentioned before, ignoring a hard truth doesn't make it any less true. In this case, ignoring a hard truth causes the needs

14. I have used "the Church" when referring to the global body of all Christians, across denominations and cultures. For clarification purposes, it has been capitalized to indicate the universal spiritual institution founded on Christ.

of others to go ignored. How can people receive the help they need if the Church refuses to acknowledge the root of their suffering? Why would they even seek help if they are met with blame and judgment, only to leave full of shame? Ignoring the fact that mental illness is real only leads to ignoring warning signs—until the symptoms of the illness become exceptionally severe. When it comes to mental health, the stakes are high. For some, it is a matter of life and death. That means we, as Christians, have to accept that mental illness *is* real.

In many ways, society has paved the way for people to seek and find help by bringing attention to the topic of mental illness. Words like "depression" and "anxiety" have even become a part of everyday language. But because society has normalized plenty of things that go against biblical teachings, we're often cautious of anything society takes and runs with. As Christians, we are to be *in* the world but not *of* the world (Romans 12:2), so it's wise to compare societal norms to scriptural truth. But by and large, that's not what we, the Church, have done with mental health.

Now this isn't a knock on the Church. It is a call to action. I've given my life to its service, desiring to love others as we are called to do as Christians. But that makes me all the more passionate that we need to right the ship. When modern day society made moves to dissolve the stigma around mental illness, especially after the pandemic, the Church held onto it. So, people have been left to seek secular guidance from society rather than Christian wisdom from the Church.

Perhaps it's a fear of anything promoted by society that's kept the Church from dissolving the stigma around mental health. Perhaps it's a general aversion to change and allegiance to the way things have always been. Regardless of the reason, there are some unfounded teachings about mental illness that still circulate in church circles. Maybe you've heard them—sayings like, *If you are depressed, that means you are in sin. Fix your sin, and your depression will go away.* Or, *If you are anxious, you are under a spiritual attack. It's not of you; it's of the devil.* Or, *If you are suicidal, go pray so they can cast the demons out of you.* While these may be the case in *certain* circumstances, this mentality should not be used as a general rule of thumb to judge. At that point, these sayings become no more than myths—beliefs that pretty much everyone accepts as true, but in the end, turn out to be false. Furthermore, these aren't helpful in the immediate nor the long haul, to say the least.

Most importantly, guidance on mental health was actually the Church's to offer in the first place, because good mental health is not just God-given, but it is also God-ordained. Along with *power* and *love*, God has given us the gift of a *sound mind*, as Scripture tells us in the first chapter of 2 Timothy: "For God hath not given us the spirit of fear; but of power, and of love, and of a sound mind." (v. 7). I like how the Amplified Bible puts it: "For God did not give us a spirit of timidity or cowardice or fear, but [He has given us a spirit] of power and of love and of sound judgment and personal discipline [abilities that result in a calm, well-balanced mind and self-control]." A sound, well-balanced, calm, and controlled mind is God-given.

But in this life and world, it is possible for our minds to become *not sound*—so, as Scripture tells us, we must heal it through renewal: "And do not be conformed to this world [any longer with its superficial values and customs], but be transformed and progressively changed [as you mature spiritually] by the renewing of your mind [focusing on godly values and ethical attitudes], so that you may prove [for yourselves] what the will of God is, that which is good and acceptable and perfect [in His plan and purpose for you]" (v. 12, Amplified Bible).

Why else would Romans tell us we must *renew* our mind? We must heal it from toxic patterns of thought to return it to—or, take back—its state of soundness. If we want to follow God's perfect will, renewing our mind is imperative. There's just no way around it. It's a nuclear part of the equation needed to unlock the understanding of God's will for our lives.

And Romans isn't the only book that makes this clear. 2 Corinthians 10 is ever more direct and adamant: "The weapons of our warfare are not physical [weapons of flesh and blood]. Our weapons are divinely powerful for the destruction of fortresses. We are destroying sophisticated arguments and every exalted and proud thing that sets itself up against the [true] knowledge of God, and we are taking every thought and purpose captive to the obedience of Christ, being ready to punish every act of disobedience, when your own obedience [as a church] is complete" (vv. 4-6).

These Scriptures intertwine in a beautiful way, providing a continuous thread and step-by-step process to getting your mind to where God always intended it to be. First, no fear! God has given us a sound mind. And if we need help finding and fulfilling God's will? Then we renew our mind. That's how we find it again. It won't be easy, because the mind is a battleground. The powers, principalities, and princes of darkness are going to do whatever possible to work against us so we don't renew our minds and thus find God's will.

So what do we do when that attack does come? Because it definitely will. We become gladiators of our mind's protection. We identify the proud, haughty, twisted arguments that the enemy raises within us to knock down God's truth, and we go against them. We do so full force and fury, grabbing that loser and shoving it down headfirst to bite the dust at Jesus' feet. And stay down!

Society and culture have taken the concepts of mental health and waved it as their own banner, but it is actually ours—the

Church's! God-given, and God-ordained. And we need not fear anything that God gives us. After all, He has *not* given us a spirit of fear.

I experienced depression firsthand, to the point that suicidal thoughts became one of my symptoms. Once my illness was given a name, I became motivated to heal in light of the common misconceptions I'd always heard. Thanks to my discerning midwife, her diagnosis, and the lovingly unrelenting messages I received from her thereafter, I became keenly aware of just how serious mental illness is. Since then, I've learned how depression, suicidal thoughts, anxiety, grief, and stress—all of which have touched my life in one way or another—affect mental health. While I can speak to them from my own personal experience, the facts about these five words commonly associated with mental illness speak for themselves.

Mental Health Lingo

When we talk about mental health, it's important to have a few definitions handy. A fairly standard definition of mental health is "the overall wellness of how you think, behave and manage your feelings."[15] A *mental health issue* is often temporary or passing, whereas a *mental health illness* is long-lasting and clinically diagnosable.

For the most part, mental health *condition*, *disorder*, or *illness* mean the same thing; they're just used in different settings. The medical world, for example, typically refers to a mental *illness* as a mental *disorder*. The general public, on the other hand, tends to use mental *condition* in everyday conversation. For whatever

15. Mayo Clinic Staff. "Mental Health: Overcoming the Stigma of Mental Illness." *Mayo Clinic*, October 14, 2022. https://www.mayoclinic.org/healthy-lifestyle/adult-health/in-depth/mental-health/art-20044098.

reason, mental *illness* often carries more of a stigma than mental *disorder*. But since we're in the business of breaking down barriers and dissolving the stigma around mental health, I don't discriminate with these words.

If you enjoy using the left side of your brain—those of you math-minded, science-oriented readers—you will have a special appreciation for the rest of this chapter. To all you liberal arts lovers: hang with me. We'll use more of the right side of our brains in the next chapter.

First, we're going to start with some facts. After all, the easiest way to debunk a myth is to illuminate the truth.

Depression

What is depression?

Depression can be both a mental health issue and a mental illness—the difference between the two being time.

If we begin by looking at the word "depression"—even before looking at any extensive scientific or psychological research—you can almost pull the words "deep" and "rest" right from it. Though those two words share no etymological origin in a historical or linguistic sense, they often appear together metaphorically and poetically—and with good reason. Your being requires rest. God created us to need rest to function, to live, to survive. But when your being's plea for rest goes ignored, depression gains a foothold.

Looking back at the explanation I gave to my midwife about all that I was feeling and thinking, I can see that what I gave her was a list of symptoms of depression. Depression entails losing interest in day-to-day activities, and it negatively impacts those activities. Someone with depression may feel hopeless, become frustrated super easily, or get overwhelmed by feelings of guilt.

Your energy levels plummet, your appetite may swivel between eating too much or too little, and your sleep patterns aren't really patterns. You could sleep too much or too little. All of this depends on how depression affects a person, but they are all signs of depression. If symptoms are severe enough, a diagnosis can be made after only two weeks—which tells you how serious health professionals are taking this.[16]

How common is depression?

Depression is by far one of the most common mental illnesses. The Institute of Health Metrics and Evaluation estimates 280 million people have depression. Worldwide, they estimate 5% of adults have depression.[17] In 2023, 18.1% of American adolescents (that's twelve to seventeen year olds) had a major depressive episode.[18]

What causes depression?

The causes of depression is a tricky topic because this isn't a one-size-fits-all situation. One recurring element in research is the hypothalamic-pituitary-adrenal (HPA) axis, which helps manage your mood, immune system, energy levels, and even digestion. It plays a major role in your body's stress response. If it becomes dysregulated, so do lots of other things in your body. Stress is overwhelmingly cited as a reason your HPA axis gets off kilter,

---

16. National Institute of Mental Health. *Depression*. Bethesda, MD: U.S. Department of Health and Human Services, National Institutes of Health, 2022. https://www.nimh.nih.gov/health/publications/depression.

17. Institute for Health Metrics and Evaluation (IHME). *GBD Results*. Seattle, WA: IHME, University of Washington, 2024. Available from https://vizhub.healthdata.org/gbd-results/.

18. Substance Abuse and Mental Health Services Administration. *Results from the 2023 National Survey on Drug Use and Health (NSDUH): Key Substance Use and Mental Health Indicators in the United States*. PEP24-07-021. Rockville, MD: U.S. Department of Health and Human Services, July 2024. https://www.samhsa.gov/data/sites/default/files/NSDUH%202023%20Annual%20Release/2023-nsduh-main-highlights.pdf.

which links stress directly to depression.[19] Your microbiome, any inflammation, and even television and cellphone usage are also documented causes that affect depression.[20]

Extensive research has been conducted on how major life changes or significant stress in early years affect adults later in life. *Brain Sciences*, an international journal on neuroscience, published a literature review just a few years ago that summarized research on depression from different fields of study. Neurology, psychology, public health, genetics, and several others—they ran the gamut.

In it, they make a point to address that "exposure to harmful determinants, such as stress" during adolescent years "can place an individual on a trajectory of depression in adulthood or later life." They go on to state firmly, "When an individual is exposed to harmful determinants during critical periods and is also genetically predisposed to depression."[21] We are all susceptible to experiencing depression, but genetics and even certain biological factors can make some of us more predisposed to it than others. I don't relay this to deliver bad news; I relay it as educational news. Knowing this can help us take a closer look at ourselves and pay closer attention to others—with a goal of helping.

19. E. P. Bertollo, M. Tanaka, C. B. Lamas, et al., "Hypothalamus-Pituitary-Adrenal and Gut-Brain Axes in Depression," Frontiers in Neuroscience, published March 2025, https://www.frontiersin.org/journals/neuroscience/articles/10.3389/fnins.2025.1541075/full.

20. Y. Zhou, D. Wang, L. Zhou, et al., "The Relationship Between Screen Time and Depression: A Systematic Review of Studies in Youth," Frontiers in Psychiatry 13 (2022): 981511, https://pmc.ncbi.nlm.nih.gov/articles/PMC9815119/.

21. Remes, Olli, José Francisco, and Peter Templeton. "Biological, Psychological, and Social Determinants of Depression: A Review of Recent Literature." *Brain Sciences* 11, no. 12 (December 2021): 1633. https://www.ncbi.nlm.nih.gov/pmc/articles/PMC8699555/.

Suicide

What is suicide?

Suicide is a symptom of depression. When depression goes untreated, the risk of suicide increases—in addition to the risk of substance abuse and anxiety.[22]

I am a prime example here. Trauma in my early life had already made me more susceptible to depression as an adult. This went from bad to worse. And I was left with an untreated and unresolved depression, compounding the risk for me to have suicidal thoughts.

However, people with depression are not the only ones who are at risk for suicide. The National Institute of Mental Health cites people who have chronic pain; a family history of a mental disorder, substance use, or suicide; or witness violence in their family can also be at risk. The death of a loved one, financial struggles, relationship difficulties, bullying, and harassment are all risk factors as well.[23]

Who experiences suicidal thoughts?

The statistics for suicide in our generation are extreme. Over 700,000 deaths are attributed to suicide every year. For fifteen- to nineteen-year-olds, suicide is ranked as the fourth leading cause of death.[24] The *fourth*. And contrary to popular Church opinion, depression and suicide are not exclusive to sin, nor the demon-possessed. The statistics for pastoral suicide are *alarming*.

---

22. Imbd.

23. National Institute of Mental Health. *Frequently Asked Questions About Suicide*. Pub ID NIMH-23-MH-6389, revised March 2023. Bethesda, MD: National Institute of Mental Health, U.S. Department of Health and Human Services, 2023. https://www.nimh.nih.gov/health/publications/suicide-faq. Accessed June 10, 2025.

24. World Health Organization. *Depressive Disorder (Depression)*. Fact sheet, March 31, 2023. Geneva: World Health Organization. https://www.who.int/news-room/fact-sheets/detail/depression.

Almost one in five ministers in the U.S. report having considered self-harm or suicide.[25] We are losing strong leaders to mental illnesses. These numbers reveal a terribly heartbreaking reality.

What causes increased risk of suicide?

There's a lot to unpack with the risk of suicide—a topic the Bible doesn't shy away from. Great figures of the Bible who were dedicated to the Lord—prophets, kings, apostles—were not excused from mental illnesses. For now, I want to briefly mention one: Elijah, a prophet of the Lord.

After a series of what I can only imagine to be exhausting events, Elijah had come to the end of his rope. It seems from Scripture that he felt fear, hurt, loneliness, sadness, guilt, and shame. Under a tree in the middle of the wilderness, he sat down and prayed to die: "He came to a broom bush, sat down under it and prayed that he might die. 'I have had enough, Lord,' he said. 'Take my life.'" Elijah, a prophet of our almighty God, wished for death.

We'll get into the details that led up to this point later, but what I want to point out right now is God's response to Elijah's suicidal thoughts. God sent an angel to care for Elijah, bringing him food and water. The angel prompted Elijah to eat—not once, but twice—ensuring Elijah regained his strength to continue on his journey.

To really simplify this, Elijah ate, drank, and napped. God cared for his physical needs and revived his strength for a forty-day journey up a mountain, the meeting place with God. When he arrived and went to hide in a cave, God began caring for his mind and heart. He asked, "Elijah! Why are you here?" Of course our

25. Barna Group. "Pastors, Too, Grapple with Thoughts of Suicide, Self-Harm." *Barna*, September 12, 2024. https://www.barna.com/research/pastors-thoughts-suicide-self-harm/.

omniscient God knew the answer. But seemingly, Elijah hadn't exteriorized the fear that was driving his despair and anguish.

The next part of the story is the one that touches me the most. God then had Elijah seek for Him through a series of amazing signs. Elijah witnessed an earthquake, a fire, and a wind so strong it shattered rocks. But God was not in any of these. Instead, He was present in a gentle whisper, a still, small voice within the silence. God knew that helping Elijah out of that deathly state of mind was to care for him—first by replenishing his bodily needs, then by providing calming comfort and safety—all while asking the reflective question, "Why are you here?"

God cared for him and brought him back to life both figuratively and literally. God knew what Elijah needed to be revived. God has entrusted us, the Church, to do the same for those like Elijah, to extend care for those who need it.

Though its culmination point was brought on the second time I gave birth, I did not get to a deftly depleted state overnight. Depletion had long been in the making. For years, I had been giving from what I didn't have, running myself completely dry. Carlos and I had been in ministry for over a decade, going where we felt called and doing as we sensed God leading us. But somewhere along the way, I'd decided to avoid rest, even though God places incredibly high value on rest. I had not learned that "no" is not a bad word. My heart was in the right place, as is the case for most people in ministry.

Unfortunately, this is a common pattern of those who are in ministry. We want so badly to give and do and tackle and help, all in the name of the Lord. But oftentimes, we exhaust ourselves without even realizing we're depleted. So we end up trying to give from nothing—because we've nothing left to give. Like Elijah, great leaders in the Church are exhausting themselves. Unlike

Elijah, they are not receiving the care they need. The enemy has managed to silence us from getting help when we need it—and we cannot continue to remain silent.

Anxiety

What is anxiety?

Anxiety is a natural response in life. The Mental Health Foundation defines it as "a common emotional state characterised by feelings of unease, such as worry or fear, that can range from mild to severe. Most people feel anxious from time to time."[26] We'd consider that a mental health challenge. In fact, it's the most common mental health challenge diagnosed today.[27] But it can progress to a mental illness. Anxiety is no longer so much a passing response you experience every now and then but becomes a constant state of life. Fear and worry take precedence in your life, becoming persistent and overwhelming. Anxiety can be severe enough to cause panic attacks, episodes when fear skyrockets within just minutes. Not shockingly, depression is linked to anxiety.

How serious is anxiety?

With two PhDs and a certificate from Harvard, Dr. John Delony has translated psychological research on anxiety into practical applications as a mental health expert. In his book *Redefining Anxiety*, he writes, "For the majority of people who face anxiety, the truth is simpler than we think: *anxiety is an alarm*. It's a

---

26. Mental Health Foundation. "What Is Anxiety?" *Mental Health Awareness Week 2023 Report*. Accessed July 24, 2025. https://www.mentalhealth.org.uk/our-work/public-engagement/mental-health-awareness-week/anxiety-report/what-anxiety.
27. Anxiety and Depression Association of America. *Facts & Statistics*. Anxiety Disorders—Facts & Statistics. Accessed June 25, 2025. https://adaa.org/understanding-anxiety/facts-statistics.

signal—nothing more and nothing less. Anxiety is simply our body's way of telling us something is wrong." He certainly isn't minimizing anxiety. It's concerned him enough that he's devoted much of his professional career to it. He's saying it's necessary to pay attention to it. And Dr. Delony—a professed Christian—states clearly that "anxiety is *real*."

What is anxiety's relationship to mental health?

Mayo Clinic lists "feeling nervous, restless or tense" and "having the urge to avoid things that trigger anxiety" in their list of symptoms of anxiety. The tipping point is when anxiety sticks around and starts messing with your daily life. At that point, anxiety can be clinically diagnosed as various types involving different kinds of phobias, social fears, separation worries, but there are also other types of anxiety that don't fall into a specific category.

Generalized anxiety can actually involve ordinary or routine circumstances—not just out-of-the-ordinary life moments—and the worry and circumstance may be disproportionate to each other. It's also possible that someone's anxiety might not check all the boxes for a specific type of anxiety disorder. But just because the symptoms don't match up with a particular type doesn't make it any less real. In those instances, a specified or unspecified anxiety disorder may be at play.[28] Anxiety is no less serious than any other mental health issue or challenge, which is why we need to address it.

---

28. Mayo Clinic Staff. "Anxiety Disorders – Symptoms and Causes." *Mayo Clinic*. Last reviewed March 19, 2024. https://www.mayoclinic.org/diseases-conditions/anxiety/symptoms-causes/syc-20350961.

Grief

What is grief?

Like anxiety, grief is part of being human. It is a natural response to the heartbreaks of this world. Grief comes from experiencing a significant loss. It is emotionally taxing, and grief felt deeply is even physically painful. It is not limited to the death of a loved one. We grieve the loss of a relationship, the end of a marriage, the loss of a job or home, the deterioration of health.

In *Prodigal Heart*, I wrote about my own experience with grief when my father died. I felt a deep, penetrating pain in my heart, the culprit of which was losing my dad. I cried constantly, screamed sometimes, and felt as though I were falling into a sinkhole of despair. I remember feeling like the pain was so great that I was drowning in it. Grief, I have found, changes over time—but it does not end.

How long does grief last?

The initial period of grief is referred to as acute grief. Grief in the weeks after a loss, or months following the loss of a loved one, is intense. Pain, shock, disbelief, difficulty focusing, fatigue, loss of appetite, and overwhelming sadness are all part of it. Acute grief will then transition to what's called adaptive grief, when you're able to re-engage in life a bit more. Adaptive progresses to integrated grief—the grief you carry throughout life. You share an ever-present existing bond with the person who has passed away, and grief becomes part of life.

Waves of grief can swell after the acute grief period—sometimes without warning. They aren't always high tide waves. They can be tidal waves, intense waves that take you by surprise. But they are a normal part of grief, even long after the loss has happened. Grief is tricky. Sneaky almost. It does not follow a fixed timeline or play by anyone's rules. What makes grief all the more complex is that everyone responds to it differently. Grief's intensity and timeframe are individual, as is the way a person responds to their grief.

What is grief's relationship to mental health?

Grief absolutely affects our mental health. Acute grief mirrors mental illness symptoms in that it affects your mood, concentration, sleep, energy levels, and appetite. It can become a mental illness. Grief that remains disabling for an extended period of time is clinically known as prolonged grief. Grief, especially in the acute phase, can also reignite a mental illness like depression or anxiety. These are some of the many reasons that knowing how to appropriately take care of yourself and support others during grief is critical. (More on this later.)

Stress

What is stress?

Cleveland Clinic defines stress as "the natural reaction your body has when changes or challenges occur. It can result in many different physical, emotional and behavioral responses. Everyone experiences stress from time to time."[29] Stress becomes dangerous, however, when "time to time" becomes constant. On its face, stress may seem to pale in comparison to, say, depression, because similar to anxiety and grief, experiencing stress is a natural part of the human condition. But also like anxiety and grief, too much stress can have drastic negative effects.

---

29. Cleveland Clinic. *Stress*. Cleveland, OH: Cleveland Clinic, n.d. https://my.clevelandclinic.org/health/diseases/11874-stress.

When does stress become dangerous?

Stress is commonly called the "silent killer." Because people can technically live with high levels of stress, they often do, never recognizing how detrimental it can be. I have definitely done this in certain seasons of my own life. It's remarkably easy to become accustomed to chronic stress and learn to just live with it. But chronic stress—we're talking high levels for a prolonged period of time—can have long-term consequences that aren't obvious in the immediate. That kind of stress quietly damages our bodies.

Stress has cycles that, if not completed, can wreak havoc on our bodies, minds, and emotions. (More on this in the following chapter.) Quick science lesson: During a stressful situation, your body releases cortisol and adrenaline. This is your body's way of helping you survive. It's an entirely normal response, and it's how we're designed. But we aren't designed to live with constant shots of those two hormones—which is what happens when we live in a constant state of stress. This is a true case of having too much of a good thing.

When your body consistently pumps out cortisol and adrenaline for an extended period of time, the hormones can harm your blood vessels, cause plaque to build up in your arteries, and raise your blood pressure. But it doesn't stop there. An article in *Frontiers in Oncology* defines chronic stress as "an emotional experience that occurs when people encounter something they cannot adapt to." We may think we've adapted to whatever recurring, stress-inducing situation we've found ourselves in, but "survival" isn't synonymous with "adapted."

When the warning signs aren't necessarily visible, it's easy to overlook the risks. But beyond cardiovascular concerns (as if those aren't enough), stress depletes our immune system, promotes cancer development, fuels its progression, and then feeds tumors.[30] One of the first points oncologists make to cancer patients is to avoid stress *as much as possible*. Research repeatedly proves that "chronic stress increases the risk of a variety of diseases, such as cardiovascular disease, depression, endocrine disease, inflammation and cancer."[31]

What is stress's relationship to mental health?

Remember the HPA axis? The thing that plays a major role in our bodies' stress response? When it's overstimulated by chronic stress, the axis flares up. It doesn't get a chance to regulate because it's overworked. So chronic stress not only worsens mental health, but it can also create a mental health condition. As our earlier mentioned *Brain Sciences* article explains, "When the stress is high or lasts for a long period of time, this may negatively impact the brain." In layman's terms, stress affects the brain's pathways and increases inflammation—both of which can lead to depression.

You've probably also heard of post-traumatic stress disorder (PTSD), which is a "condition that can develop following a physical, psychological, or sexual trauma"[32]—or as *Neuroscience and Biobehavioral Review* says, it can "follow exposure to extreme stressful situations.[33] Soldiers, for example, often experience PTSD when they return from war. Someone with PTSD often startles easily and frequently, relives the traumatic event, withdraws from others, and numbs their emotions. After someone

30. For more, search "chronic stress" in the Nationally Library of Medicine.

31. Hong, Hao, Min Ji, and Donglai Lai. "Chronic Stress Effects on Tumor: Pathway and Mechanism." *Frontiers in Oncology*11 (December 20, 2021): 738252. https://pubmed.ncbi.nlm.nih.gov/34988010/.

32. Maeng, Lisa Y., and Mohammed R. Milad. "Post-Traumatic Stress Disorder: The Relationship Between the Fear Response and Chronic Stress." *Chronic Stress* 1 (June 27, 2017): 1–13. https://pubmed.ncbi.nlm.nih.gov/32440579/.

33. Hong, Hao, Min Ji, and Donglai Lai.

experiences violence or trauma, they can actually *develop* chronic stress and PTSD.[34] But because PTSD is a condition you can develop, it's also able to be prevented—if it's caught early enough.[35] Again, this is information we need to promote mental health education across the board.

It was Moses' curiosity that brought him to the presence of the Lord.

When God called Moses to bring the Israelites out of Egypt, He spoke to him from a burning bush. Moses was working at his day job—tending to his father-in-law's sheep—when he saw a bush on fire. The way Scripture reads, he wasn't so much curious as to why the bush was on fire as to why it didn't burn up. He thought, "I will go over and see this strange sight—why the bush does not burn up" (Exodus 3:3).

From the bush, God said, "I have indeed seen the misery of my people in Egypt. I have heard them crying out because of their slave drivers, and I am concerned about their suffering. So I have come down to rescue them from the hand of the Egyptians and to bring them up out of that land into a good and spacious land, a land flowing with milk and honey" (vv. 7-8). Then, He told Moses to bring the Israelites out of Egypt. As you might imagine, Moses had several questions at this. He seemed concerned he wasn't the man for the job, asking, "Who am I that I should go to Pharaoh and bring the Israelites out of Egypt?" (v. 11). He asked who he was to say sent him (v. 13), and he expressed concern as

34. Saunders, Emily F. "Introduction." *Journal of Clinical Psychiatry* 77, no. 5 (May 2016): 672. https://doi.org/10.4088/JCP.16f10815.

35. Howlett, Jennifer R., and Murray B. Stein. "Prevention of Trauma and Stressor-Related Disorders: A Review." *Neuropsychopharmacology* 41, no. 1 (January 2016): 357–69. https://doi.org/10.1038/npp.2015.261.

to if anyone would believe him (4:1). But God answered all of his questions with clarity and direction.

Questions are a mark of a curious person. Asking questions is how we gain knowledge, discover information, and develop relationships. Since my diagnosis, I've asked lots of questions about mental health, and I've learned more through professional therapy and my own research. I encourage you to do the same, beyond what I've already shared. I consider the information I've included in this chapter to be a starting point. There's still much more to learn and uncover. Ask questions. Be curious. Pray for God to give you clarity. If you ask God for wisdom, He will give it to you generously (James 1:5).

Now, more than ever, we must destigmatize mental health—conditions, illnesses, disorders, all of it—especially in communities of faith. Our generation is experiencing more of these issues and illnesses than any other generation that has come before. They aren't new illnesses, but they are rapidly increasing and wreaking havoc on us—younger, older, and everyone in between. The statistics should sound all kinds of sirens that people are in great need of help.

The numbers do not allow us to simply argue mental illness out of existence, and we cannot continue to ignore it.

CHAPTER 4

CHOOSING TO HEAL (AND CARVING A PATH)

Healing is a choice—a path that must be chosen. The path itself is the healing process, one to be carved on the journey that heals. It is a path intentionally chosen, forged, and carved. After the birth of my second child, all of my being needed healing. The hurt I'd been carrying was both old and new. And quite frankly, I'd been ignoring the subtle alarms my body had been giving me for years. It took the immense act of birthing two humans in two and a half years to trigger a response in me.

I was certain that if my midwife was correct and there was a way out, I wanted to know how I could make my exit. I knew that if I wanted to heal, I had to quit hiding how I was feeling and shake off the shame I'd been carrying for so long. I wasn't sure how to do that, which is where therapy came in. Through therapy, with a Bible-centered, Spirit-filled Christian therapist (as therapy should be led by the Holy Spirit), I began to understand my own personal history with depression. I started to see how it had taken shape over the course of my life and progressively gotten worse—because I had not attended to healing it.

Imagine that you break your leg. Instead of going to the doctor, you decide to ignore your leg. *It's probably fine*, you think. You're in a searing amount of pain, but you don't have any idea how to make it stop. *The pain probably isn't even real*, you think. You try to go on about life, but your broken leg keeps you from being able to. It interferes with everything you try to do. *I just need to power through*, you think. Rather than getting better, your leg seems to get progressively worse.

Right now, you're thinking, *I would never ignore a broken leg*. If you actually broke your leg, you would do everything it took to head straight to the ER for x-rays, CT scans, physical exams, a cast, and surgery if need be. But what about a pain that's not so jarring or one that doesn't come on all at once?

So, imagine you wake up one morning and have a tinge of pain in your right side. *It's probably fine*, you think. And it is. The pain isn't so bad—until later that evening. It seems to have slowly increased during the day. *The pain probably isn't even real*, you think. Sure enough, when you wake up the next morning, the pain seems to have dissipated overnight. In a few days, however, the pain is back—with a vengeance. *I just need to power through*, you think. But this time, there is no powering through the pain needling in your side, so you go to the doctor. Turns out, you have a kidney stone.

One way or another, you wind up at the doctor in both scenarios. When we get injured or sick, we go to a medical professional so that we can heal. But just as a doctor formulates a path for physical healing, a therapist does the same thing for your mental health. Maybe you're deep in the throes of depression. Maybe your worries have evolved to fear that's crippling at times. Maybe stress never leaves your side anymore. These are all valid reasons to visit a Christian faith-based therapist.

But it doesn't take the mental equivalent of a broken leg or a kidney stone to go to a therapist either. Much like you go to a doctor for a physical exam to stay up-to-date on your physical health, you can and should do the same with your mental health. Maybe you're dealing with a stressful situation or grieving an expected loss. Maybe you've always been a little on the nervous side, sometimes fixating on your worries a little too much. Maybe making decisions is sometimes more challenging than they should be. A therapist can help with all these concerns—before they develop and escalate. The point? The healing journey is best navigated alongside the guidance of a professional.

When we go to the doctor, we don't hesitate to bring that up in conversation. In fact, if we make mention of a doctor appointment at church, someone will often offer to pray on the spot. Similarly, if we can openly discuss healing in communities of faith, then we can openly discuss healing that is grounded in Christian principles. With empathy and understanding, this is a much needed area that the church can step into, offering good mental health practices to those in ministry *and* those seeking help.

Casting blame and causing guilt have no place in those practices and only fosters an environment of shame. As a part of the church, we can and should embrace the hurting with meekness, even when we do not understand someone's situation or perhaps approve of how they're handling it. The role of the church is to serve and support others practically and sacrificially, and being a helping hand is a deeply biblical message. We are to come alongside others in their struggles, help where we are able, and love with our actions.[36]

Through this lens, we can approach healing with a Christian perspective of truth and love—and carve our path to healing.

---

36. "Carry each other's burdens, and in this way you will fulfill the law of Christ" (Galatians 6:2); "Do not withhold good from those to whom it is due, when it is in your power to act" (Proverbs 3:27); and "If anyone has material possessions and sees a brother or sister in need but has no pity on them, how can the love of God be in that person? Dear children, let us not love with words or speech but with actions and in truth" (1 John 3:17-18).

Depression

Being diagnosed with depression made mental illness much more real to me. Having been fed all the common misconceptions about mental health before my diagnosis, I had believed some of the unfounded teachings about mental illness. I could pretend I was fine long enough to make it through the day, and at times, I made myself believe I actually might be. I knew enough to recognize that I was not functioning at full capacity, to say the least, but I didn't have the knowledge, tools, or resources to understand the seriousness of my illness. My diagnosis changed all that.

Our Lesson: We need to heal our depression.

You can basically boil all the scientific depression jargon down to one main cause: a lack of basic needs. First, we have physical needs—eating, drinking, sleeping, having a roof over our heads. These are our most basic needs, what we require to survive. Next, we need safety—from violence, natural disasters, or danger in general. We desire stability and want protection. Then, we need to feel as though we belong. God created humans to be in community with one another, so we need companionship, love, support, and connection. Proverbs says, "A friend is always loyal, and a brother is born to help in time of need" (17:17, NLT). We need to be seen, valued, and accepted by our core group, our inner circle of people. When our basic needs aren't met, we become prone to depression.

To say that someone's depression will "go away" if they just "fix their sin" is a misconstrued idea. The Bible does speak to the relationship between sin, guilt, and emotional well-being, but not in such simplistic terms. Sin can cause emotional suffering, but not all emotional suffering is caused by sin. In the book of John,

Jesus plainly corrects the assumption that suffering is always tied to personal sin (9:2-3).

Applying the Lesson: Healing your depression is possible. Jesus Himself was well acquainted with the hurts of this world, "a man of suffering, and familiar with pain" (Isaiah 53:3). Feeling sadness, experiencing symptoms of depression, and sensing dissatisfaction in your soul are all part of being human. God created us to feel emotion—and even Jesus wept (John 11:35).

Feeling as though you're searching for a remedy that seems ever-evading is valid. But if we pay close attention to what Jesus did in the midst of His own sadness and suffering, His first response was always to turn to God, the only one who can carry the heavy burdens of this world. He stayed in constant communication with God, keeping His sight set on fulfilling His purpose. Jesus modeled for us how to approach our suffering: closely communing with God.

A remedy will come by way of healing—and healing is powerful when it's done with God, the divine healer.

Suicide

A few years ago, I heard about a much beloved pastor's wife who took her life after battling postpartum depression, PTSD, and anxiety. My heart hurt for her family—her husband and five children, the youngest of which was only months old. That news hit me hard because I knew that could have been me just a couple years prior. When I told my mom the heartbreaking news, she shared with me that she had been tempted to end her life when she was a teenager. She'd been abandoned by her mother and orphaned as a young girl. She felt unwanted and saw no hope.

During our phone conversation, a voice on the other end of the phone—someone visiting my parents in Puerto Rico—delivered more devastating news. My mom's dear friend and coworker had passed away the night before. She had taken her life.

In that moment, I felt as if time stood still for a moment. Like when a scene in a movie just stops everything, and only the main character remains animated. I saw four women: myself, my mother before me, a close friend, and a distant minister's wife. We all loved and feared the Lord. We all knew the truth. And in that same space, we all battled suicide. Sadly, for two of the four of us, the battle waging in our minds won out.

Our Lesson: Don't take your life!

Our battles are real, and life is so fragile. A moment can change a lifetime. I am thankful my heart is still beating, that I am alive to see the glory of the Lord in the land of the living. I serve a God who has saved me from myself time and time again. He has kindly restored my broken, shattered pieces and created what I can recognize as beautiful in myself now. I am a walking example of restoration.

To those who may be struggling, know that your tribulation will not last forever. Rejection, trauma, pain, wounds, and hopelessness can make it seem as though there is no hope—but you are still here, and that alone is evidence of hope. I too am evidence of hope. God loves you, and He is able to save and restore your life as well. You are brave, valiant, spectacular in unique ways. Don't let the enemy lie to you about your value.

I pray you will quickly learn to see each day as worth living. Be patient. Hold on a little longer. Don't let life end before its time. You may think, *that's easy for you to say when you're not in my position.* But I will say that it hasn't always been so easy for me to admit I was suicidal. When I realized that my story might give even one person hope to hold on, to see what God can do, then I knew I would tell it to the masses.

Applying the Lesson: Surviving suicide.

If you are having or if you ever have thoughts about ending your life, tell someone *immediately*. As in, this very moment. Ask that they not leave you alone. Even if that seems dramatic or unnecessary to you right now, it's much better to tell someone than to risk anything at all. Then, talk to one of your healthcare providers *immediately*. Be open and honest with them, and don't hold anything back. They can help create a personalized plan for you and refer you to a mental health professional (like my midwife did for me).

> If, in this moment, you are having thoughts of ending your life, stop for a minute. Pause your reading, and call the suicide hotline in your area. If you have a smartphone, scan this code with your camera. It will give you a list of numbers in your area to call—and call now. This book will be waiting for you to pick it up when you're ready again.

For those who are supporting someone who is having suicidal thoughts, be absolutely certain they have sought the help of a mental health provider. If you sense they are in immediate danger, don't leave them alone. Call a provider, emergency services, or a crisis line.[37] Once they are receiving care, know that you can

37. Crisis resources: U.S.: Suicide & Crisis Lifeline, call or text 988; Substance Abuse and Mental Health Services Administration U.S. helpline, 1-800-662-HELP (4357); Canada: Talk Suicide Canada, 1-833-456-4566.

make a profound difference in their life. Be present and listen. Allow them to speak openly and talk about how they're feeling. While you may have difficulty understanding, being judgmental (if even accidentally) is unhelpful. Be careful not to minimize their experience. They need to feel connected and valued during this time, so continue checking in with them regularly, with even short "thinking of you" text messages.

As long as there is life, there is hope. Let our lives be a slap in the enemy's face, a reminder that we are still here.

Anxiety

Once upon a time, there lived a little girl whose natural disposition lent itself to being rather high strung. She was driven, and she accomplished great goals and achievements. But because she was a high achiever, she was often in situations that made her feel nervous. Contests, competitions, tryouts, playoffs, and performances layered on top of her academic work, which she took very seriously. She excelled in school and went on to earn a degree from an Ivy League university. As she grew up, she became accustomed to feeling nervous, assuming her feeling of being "overwhelmed" from time to time was just her lot in life.

This is a fictional tale, but it is a tale of truth for many people. The details may be different, but the underlying truth is there: some of us live with anxiety and never even know.

Our Lesson: Cast all your anxiety.

As we know, anxiety manifests itself in various ways. It can take the form of nerves all the way to panic attacks. These happen when the body is in such a state of fear, stress, or overwhelm that it goes into an adrenal response to that stress or trauma. A panic attack is brought on when some unforeseen fear takes us by surprise, which dysregulates the body so much that it pumps extra adrenaline into the blood.[38] Panic attacks are a glaring sign, but anxiety often goes overlooked because the warning signs aren't always so obvious. We confuse natural responses with persistent anxiety. We blame our personality or disposition, thinking we're just prone to being nervous or overwhelmed.

Just as the Bible doesn't say depression will "go away" once you've "fixed your sin," it also does not tell us we can just "pray our anxiety away." This idea hits *around* Biblical truth but not directly on it and misconstrues what is actually scriptural truth. We are absolutely called to lay our burdens on Jesus. 1 Peter 5:7 reads, "Cast all your anxiety on Him because He cares for you." The idea is that instead of carrying the weight of anxiety ourselves, we are invited to give it over to Jesus, trusting in His care, strength, and faithfulness. This has to be a constant practice. Cast *all* your anxiety. When those feelings of being unsettled, nervous, or on edge start to return, we are to go to Jesus again, giving our burdens to Him again.

Applying the Lesson: Practice calming techniques.

Anxiety can hit all of a sudden, even if you know it's been building for some time. To calm your mind and body, you can use some simple in-the-moment techniques. When anxiety hits, start by taking a big drink of water (at least ten to sixteen ounces at once). Then start to slow your breath. Inhale deeply through your nose for four seconds. Hold that breath gently for seven seconds. Then, exhale slowly through your mouth for a count of eight, allowing the tension to leave your body as you breathe out.

38. Fisher, Jennifer. 2024. "Panic Attacks: Recognizing and Managing Panic Attacks and Preventing Future Attacks." *Harvard Health Publishing*, May 24, 2024. https://www.health.harvard.edu/mind-and-mood/panic-attacks-recognizing-and-managing-panic-attacks-and-preventing-future-attacks.

Repeat this (called the four-seven-eight cycle) three or four times, focusing only on your breath and the rhythm. You can do this while your feet are planted firmly to give your body a sense of stability. Going for a walk can also help release some anxious energy stored in your muscles and give you time to arrange your thoughts.

When these techniques help in the short term, don't forget about the need for long-term healing. And continually cast your anxiety on the one who cares for you.

Grief

In the United States, Father's Day is a special holiday to honor fathers, grandfathers, and everyone who has been a father and raised a child. For those of us who have lost our fathers, it's a difficult day. Now, as I watch my kids with their dad, my husband, I see the innocence in their eyes as they enjoy spending time with dad. I am blessed that they are unfamiliar with the pain caused by an absent father, the deep wound an absent father leaves. I know my dad is with the Lord, worshiping with the angels. He's become part of the great cloud of witnesses who see us and cheer for our triumphs. While I'm on Earth, separated from Him, there will be an ache in my heart that I will carry, right there alongside my hope of heaven.

Our Lesson: Share your grief.

I spent a long time not sharing my grief. I've chosen to trust that sharing about it now might help those who are grieving know they are not alone. Everyone experiences grief at some point; it's part of being human. I share my experience with grief so that it may give you hope—because I continue to hold onto hope. God created us for community, and we are meant to have each other in seasons of grief. He also sent the Holy Spirit—the Comforter—to Earth, to help us through them.

There is no reason to hide our pain and sadness. I have learned that I often feel grief in my chest, as though lava inside my chest burns to come out—and I've learned to let it. Jesus did not hide His tears when Lazarus died—and He even knew He was going to resurrect Lazarus. It's important that we release our feelings as well. Even when in the presence of others. In fact, our children need to see what releasing emotions in a *healthy* way looks like. Our children cannot be our pillars, and we should not turn to them as sources of strength. But without ever seeing how you express emotions, they will grow up unsure how to handle their own emotions.

Even when you expect grief to come in waves, it will likely still take you by surprise when the next wave comes. Sadness over your loss will return, but you will also progressively feel peace again. You will always miss the one you have loved and lost, but the pain lessens with time. The loss becomes part of you, a part you're able to honor with a peace gained over time.

Applying the Lesson:
Bridge the gap between the grieving and non-grieving.

The wide gap that opens between the grieving and non-grieving is often created by non-grievers' misunderstanding of grief. I was told once that people will say some of the strangest, most unhelpful things when you're grieving—and boy is this true.

When you talk to a griever, give your words much thought in real time. Comments like, "I can't imagine what you're going through," only make them feel further isolated. Avoid saying anything that is dismissive of their pain, such as, "They're in a better place now." Yes, as believers we have the assurance of heaven. But it is also true that the separation from a loved one causes a profound longing and hurt for those of us in this world. Yes, the joy of the Lord is our strength, *and* we still hurt in this life. Avoid peppering them with a stream of questions. Grief drains energy, and their job is not to educate. Your job is to comfort and support. Be present beside them and give them room to grieve.

The shock that loss brings with it can make a griever's soul feel numb, as though they are drifting through a dream or living someone else's life, which is incredibly disorienting. They often move from not feeling anything to feeling everything—deeper pain than they've ever felt for longer than they thought possible. Don't look away from their pain. Perhaps it's because grievers are already inundated with emotions, but they can sense when someone is uncomfortable. Grievers need to be able to express their emotions openly, which requires a certain level of comfort to be expressed from you.

Grief can be exceptionally isolating because, to the griever, it can seem like no one understands what they're going through. Truth be told, you can't fully understand their loss, even if you have lost a loved one. You may have experienced grief from loss in the past, but you haven't experienced *their* grief from *their* loss. Sometimes it's helpful for grievers to hear from others about their experiences with grief. But sharing your experience with grief can also come across as though it's minimizing their loss. You haven't lived their life, had that relationship, experienced that loss. This is a delicate balance, so it's okay to ask what would be helpful. When in doubt, know that most of the time, it's the ministry of presence that best comforts those in grief. Be present, be quiet, be beside them, and give space for their grief to take the path it needs to in that moment.

God is not distant when we are in pain. In fact, He draws closer. When your heart is breaking from grief, God is *near*, and He *saves*—not always by instantly changing the situation, but by being present, offering peace, and carrying us through it.

Stress

When you spend a prolonged period in a high-stress state, your body is constantly in survival mode. *Do whatever you must to survive,* it says. *Don't let your guard down.* Out of necessity, your body develops a habit of pumping out adrenaline and cortisol. Trauma and extreme stress go hand-in-hand—with the former leading to the latter. For me, the trauma of delivering our firstborn triggered a high-stress state when I became pregnant with our second child. I had PTSD from my first delivery, and my body was unsuccessfully trying to regulate itself.

Our Lesson: Identify the deeper concern.

Stress is a common indicator of a deeper concern. In the last chapter, I mentioned that when your being's plea for rest goes ignored, depression gains a foothold. Of course, one of the most rest-depriving causes in life is stress, which is why stress can worsen mental health but also create a mental health condition. So what happens when stress and lack of rest compound? Depression *often* ensues. But we may not know it's depression, not just stress, because depression mimics stress—but in a dysregulated and prolonged form that no longer serves a healthy purpose.[39]

If you are experiencing higher-than-normal stress, something is going on that you need to pay attention to. Sensing stress is your

39. Gold, Philip. "The Relationship Between Depression and Stress." *Psychology Today*, Accessed July 27, 2025. https://www.psychologytoday.com/us/blog/next-generation-research/202402/the-relationship-between-depression-and-stress.

body's way of telling you that. You may already know what is causing your stress but you're unsure how to deal with it. Or perhaps you have no idea why you're so stressed. This is why seeking the guidance of a professional is helpful; they can help you navigate how to handle your stress and identify its cause.

In order for your body to know it doesn't have to be in survival mode anymore, it has to be convinced that the danger is over. You can try to reason with your body all day (and night) long, telling it you aren't in danger anymore, but until your body gets the message in a way it understands, stress will remain cyclical. When you lay awake at night, unable to sleep. When you sweat through your clothes as you sleep. When you jump every time a car breaks in front of you. You have to communicate in the language the body understands.

Applying the Lesson: Complete the cycle of stress.

Stress has a cycle. If that cycle does not run its course, the body has a hard time understanding it's safe and, in turn, acts out. So, you must complete the cycle of stress. This cycle begins with a *stressor*, which is "anything you see, hear, smell, touch, taste, or imagine could do you harm."[40] Stress is what happens when your body and brain shift in response to that perceived threat, in order to equip you to survive.

As humans, we have not evolved in our stress response from the days of our ancient ancestors who lived in the wild thousands of years ago. Today, our body reacts to receiving an email with bad news while sitting at an office in the same way our ancestors' body reacted if they were chased by a predatory wild animal. Not giving stress a way out of our bodies can wreak havoc on every area of our being. It can lead to burnout and often even to depression.[41]

---

40. Nagoski, Amelia. *Burnout: The Secret to Unlocking the Stress Cycle.* Ballantine Books, 2019.
41. Ibid.

Here is a basic description of what the cycle of stress is:

1. *A stressor appears.* It could be work, a family conflict, loss of money, etc.
2. *The body's stress response system turns on.* Stress hormones and extra adrenaline start flowing abundantly through your body, and your circulatory system shifts to enable you to fight or flee.
3. *The stressor is handled.* You either overcome and *fight* it (in a figurative sense, since physical aggression is usually inappropriate when the stressor does not represent imminent physical danger), or you depart and *flee* from the stressor.
4. *Close the cycle.* You tell the body it's safe—by physically moving your body, with deep breathing, by laughing or crying, in physical connection with a loved one, through creativity or with social connection.
5. *The body's rest and recovery system turns on.* You hydrate, eat nutritious food, and sleep.

Here are a few beginner messages you can send to your body in its own language that can help you complete the cycle of stress:

1. *Do some physical activity.* The best way to signal to your body that you are *running from* the stressor and *running to* safety is to engage in physical activities that elevate your heart rate and make you break a sweat continuously for twenty minutes or more—at least three times a week—or on days when you encounter many stressors.
2. *Find a safe space.* Go into your home, room, closet—wherever you feel secure. Breathe to calm your body.
3. *Express your feelings.* Laugh, cry, rejoice, shout, sing. Relax to release your stress.
4. *Eat nourishing, nutritious food.* Eat foods like green vegetables, raw fruit, and lean proteins to replenish your body. Hydrate

well, and use nutritional supplements to make up for the lack of nutrients in our modern day diets.

5. *Seek out the community of people who you love most.* Spend time with your tribe, inner circle, and faith community. Commune to comfort your body. Social media does not count! Make sure you have actual face-to-face connections.
6. *Have safe physical contact with a loved one.* Studies show that a strong hug lasting twenty seconds or more stimulates the release of oxytocin (a feel-good body-repairing hormone), lowers cortisol (stress hormone), and even helps the body to regulate blood pressure and heart rate! This kind of safe contact with a loved one or even a pet can send a message of safety to the body.[42]
7. *Sleep well.* Get at least eight hours of sleep—and more as needed. Establish a consistent bedtime routine and go to bed at the same time each night, even on weekends. Avoid screens, caffeine, and heavy meals before bed to help your body wind down naturally.

Jesus modeled how to break the cycle of stress. And we'll look at some specific biblical examples of Jesus breaking the cycle of stress in chapters to come. Throughout the Gospels, He regularly went up into the mountains or solitary places to be alone with God, especially during intense seasons of ministry or emotional strain. When He reached the place He felt safest, He was able to be with God, to lay His burdens down, to recharge. Then, He returned, renewed to continue fulfilling God's purpose. This was part of the path Jesus carved for Himself, healing in real time.

42. Eccker Eddie. "The 6-Second Kiss & the 20-Second Hug: Small Habits That Heal Big Wounds." Accessed May 19, 2025. https://www.myvc.org/post/the-6-second-kiss-the-20-second-hug-small-habits-that-heal-big-wounds#:~:text=The%20same%20goes%20for%20the,—they're%20physiological%20anchors.

PART II

A VOICE TO CRY OUT —INSIDE THE DESERT *FORMATION*

CHAPTER 5

THE COST OF HEALING

Once I accepted that I needed to heal, I knew I had to approach it with practicality moving forward—meaning, I knew I needed to take a practical approach to healing. Though I chose to heal for my own sake, I was ultimately choosing to become whole—to become the person God created me to be.

As we align ourselves with God, what He desires *for* us and *from* us becomes much clearer to see. God gave us a heart to love, a mind to reason, a soul to believe, and strength to move. He intends for us to use all four parts of ourselves—to use them well, to our full potential, and to bring Him glory. We become who God intends us to be when we heal each part of our being. And we become whole by healing.

Put bluntly, healing comes with a cost. There is no sweeping that fact under the rug or hiding it out of sight somewhere. There's just no way around it. And the thought of knowingly and voluntarily choosing to pay its cost can be daunting. *But that doesn't mean it isn't worth it.* Because I can tell you, healing *is* worth its cost.

You can prepare for some of its challenges simply by knowing to expect them. That way, when you run up against them, you won't be taken entirely by surprise. This is where my experience comes in handy: I'm going to give you a heads up on some challenges you can expect—not to scare you, but to prepare you. You can take what I've learned on my journey and use it to prepare you for your own.

Experiencing Seasons and Expecting Emotions

The third chapter of Ecclesiastes, a book of wisdom literature, begins, "There is a time for everything, and a season for every activity under the heavens" (v. 1). These words invite us to recognize that life unfolds in seasons. Joyful seasons, sad seasons, desert seasons. Seasons of abundance, seasons of little, seasons of healing.

These seasons bring emotions with them. We are to expect that seasons will change and our emotions with them. Ecclesiastes doesn't call us to escape our emotions but to embrace them as part of the God-given rhythm of being human. There is "a time to weep and a time to laugh, a time to mourn and a time to dance" (v.4), and significantly, "a time to heal" (v. 3). This passage affirms that there is time to feel every emotion—grief, anger, hope, exhaustion, joy. We are not made to stay in joy forever, nor to remain in sorrow indefinitely. They are all a part of our lived experience.

Healing is a season, and the healing process is a journey in the desert. Healing means honoring our emotions, giving them space, and trusting God in the midst of this season. In doing so, we move from resistance to acceptance, from hiding to honesty, and from survival to wholeness.

Healing Is Painful

Remember when you were a kid and you just expressed all your emotions without reservation? If you were happy, you jumped up and down. If you were sad, you cried—sometimes really loudly. If you were tired, you also probably ended up in tears. It didn't matter where you were, especially when you were really little. If you felt it, out it came. As children, we don't know how to regulate our emotions, but as we grow, we learn to manage them more effectively.

Now, as an adult, you don't burst into tears, wailing and crying when the store is out of your favorite ice cream.

But there's a difference between *regulating* your emotions and *conquering* your emotions. If you see your emotions as something to conquer, to battle and wage war against, you run the risk of avoiding, numbing, or suppressing them. Somewhere along the way between your younger years and adult life now, you may have learned to manage your emotions so that you don't feel them enough—or at all.

Letting emotions pass through our bodies is a required part of the healing process. It is essential for healing. We don't just experience emotions mentally; we feel them physically. We can identify feelings of fear, sadness, hurt, or anger by the tension in our bodies, the tightness in our chests, or the knots in our stomachs. Mental health experts will suggest not to label emotions as "bad" versus "good," but we all know an uncomfortable, painful emotion from a perfectly lovely one.

But just because we don't acknowledge uncomfortable emotions—whether by avoiding, numbing, or suppressing—doesn't mean they aren't there. Take anger, for example. We feel anger when we aren't getting something we want. You might think that if you suppress your anger down far enough or ignore it for long enough that it will just disappear. But it doesn't. It lodges itself somewhere inside you, festering until it morphs into resentment.

Unprocessed emotions, like anger, can evolve into deeper, more harmful states. Harbored hurt can become bitterness. Fear can become anxiety. Shame can become self-hatred. In the case of unprocessed fear or shame specifically, our bodies continue responding to stress—because to it, the pain is still there. So fear and shame have the potential to become anxiety or chronic stress. And if you think you can pick and choose which emotions you will feel and which ones you won't, you're wrong. Emotions don't work like that. It's all or nothing. If you set out to not feel painful emotions and work at that long enough, you will lose your ability to feel the more pleasant emotions. When you numb pain, you numb all—and that gives depression an easy entrance.

Our natural tendency is to flee from pain, which means that our natural reflex is to escape pain. But when we refuse to acknowledge painful emotions, we only hide our pain—whether from ourselves or everyone else. They end up residing in our inner selves. As pushed down or swept aside as we think they are, they're still there—hiding in our hearts, residing in our souls, weighing on our minds. Try as we might to escape them, we really just end up holding onto them, unconsciously clinging to our pain. In the end, we needlessly prolong or create even more suffering for ourselves.

So how do you let them go? Sit with your emotions, and *feel* them. Sitting with uncomfortable feelings is hard. Sometimes, it's the last thing we want to do. It certainly was for me. There were many times I lashed out at my therapist when I'd come to the end of a session, and she'd instruct me to *sit with them*—meaning, get still, be quiet, and feel the feelings, letting the pain pass through your body.

In one of those moments I got angry and lashed out, I asked her how she could ask me to sit with feelings that stemmed from horrible traumatic experiences I had as a child. Her answer stunned me, and her words remain with me to this day: *If you don't still yourself to feel them, you won't be able to figure out where it's coming from. Therefore, you won't know what it is you have to heal.* I would have given anything not to have had to go to those painful places of my soul. But that day, I understood that if I didn't go back to them, a bad thing would only become worse. I needed to make the shift and decide to *sit with them* so I could *heal them.*

When you do this, you can grab a friend whose shoulder you can cry on or a pillow whose cover you can yell into. Journal your thoughts or write a letter you never have to send. Externally processing helps bring clarity to your thoughts while also fighting an urge to suppress your emotions. Paint a picture, sketch a drawing, write a poem, sing a song. Process your emotions creatively, giving your emotions space. Feeling them allows you to let them go so they can move through and out of your body. Visualize a challenging emotion with acceptance rather than resistance, allowing the pain to pass through your body.

When we don't process our emotions, they're blocked from getting to the other side of pain. We have to allow ourselves to *feel* our emotions, so that they can *pass through* our bodies. To give our bodies a chance to regulate, we have to make room for the pain to pass through. Though that may seem counterproductive, it's actually the only way to move forward with clarity and peace. Letting emotions pass through—*feeling them fully*—allows them to move and be released, rather than being held inside and causing long-term harm. Little by little, you will feel peace again. The pain you feel initially won't last forever. And God will be with you, right in the thick of it.

Desert Cries

During their desert wanderings, the Israelites cried out to and pleaded with God multiple times. When they were scared at Mount Sinai, they felt a profound fear in the presence of God's holiness. Exodus reads, "When the people saw the thunder and lightning and heard the trumpet and saw the mountain in smoke, they trembled with fear" (20:18). God had descended on the mountain in fire, and the Earth shook beneath them. This wasn't the first time the

Israelites had seen God's display of power, of course, but they were reminded of just how small they were and just how big God is. So they cried out, begging Moses to talk to God for them. "Speak to us yourself and we will listen. But do not have God speak to us or we will die" (Exodus 20:19). Overwhelmed by God's holiness, they feared death and cried out in their distress.

Then, after creating and worshiping the golden calf, the Israelites were confronted with the weight of their betrayal and the consequences of their sin (Exodus 32–33). Moses had been on Mount Sinai, and they grew tired of waiting on him to return. In his absence, their impatience got the better of them. When Moses descended and saw they'd created an idol, he shattered the tablets in grief and anger. This was a major breach in relationship. But this moment turns out to be a turning point for the Israelites because once they realized the gravity of their sin, the people were devastated and "they began to mourn" (33:4). They cried out, fearing the thought of losing God's presence. Feeling guilty over their actions, they humbly repented.

After my therapist explained why I needed to sit with my feelings, I gained a new perspective and even a new sense of compassion for the people of Israel in the desert, which allowed me to speculate a little on what Scripture doesn't explicitly tell us. What if the Israelites' act of building that golden calf was a way to escape the silence of the desert? What if the stillness of the waiting began to create a space in which they began to *sit with* things they didn't want to feel?

Think about it. They had just left a life of multi-generational slavery full of daily abuse and trauma. All they knew was survival. Their bodies must have been in chronic stress, which had probably been present their entire life until this point. And what was their method of survival in Egypt? It was to try and blend in with Egyptian society and its way of life. Yes, they were earnestly waiting for Moses to bring them a word from God. But maybe their choice to build that calf was their way of fleeing from the pain that may have been coming to the surface while they remained still. They may not have been able to understand that the stillness was an opportunity to feel and explore their pain in order to heal it.

I could understand this, and I still understand it now. I ran from my pain for decades. I filled my silence with everything I could to drown out the sound of my hurt. Back in the Israelites' time, their escape of choice was idolatry. Today, we may escape from pain with other things that take us back to *our* Egypt—what feels familiar to us. Be it over-working, anxious-eating, substance abuse, or other addictions, behaviors like these can easily become coping mechanisms of escape from the real problem and its root issue. Humans have a tendency to flee from pain. But when we run from truth in our pain, I have found that usually reveals something more: a deep penetrating sadness.

When the Israelites learned that Aaron had passed away, they were faced with another opportunity to feel in order to heal. And they entered a season of communal grief. Aaron, the high priest and brother of Moses, had been a central spiritual leader and figure of stability throughout their journey in the wilderness. When he passed, the Israelites felt the change to come, the end of an era. "When the whole community learned that Aaron had died, all the Israelites mourned for Him thirty days" (Numbers 20:28–29). This was not a brief or private moment—it was a collective cry of sadness, a public acknowledgment of deep loss. Their mourning reflected not only personal affection for Aaron, but also a shared sense of vulnerability and change. They cried out, expressing their grief openly as one people.

This is the crying out in the desert: taking the time to sit with what you feel, letting it flow through and out of you. When the Israelites experienced painful emotions, they cried out to God. While you experience painful emotions, cry out to God. When you do, your voice becomes evidence of your healing. It will be proof that you are feeling the emotions that you must allow yourself to feel so they can pass through—an integral part of the healing process. While you are inside your desert, use your voice to cry out; release it as you release your emotions. Let your voice be the aqueduct through which God's healing waters flow.

This is *your* crying out in the desert.

Healing Is Challenging

Pain isolates us, whereas healing flourishes in connection. There is no need to heal alone. Like I mentioned before, healing is best done with a professional who can help unpack emotional pain and internal struggles. Their job is to guide us toward healing and wholeness. Making it through the door of a therapist's office can be challenging, but it is a brave, admirable move.

If the idea of a therapist is new to you, this may sound cheesy, but therapists really do give you a safe, supportive space, so you can speak openly. It is a judgement-free zone. Confidentiality is one of the most important ethical and legal principles in mental health care, so whatever you say to your therapist, stays with your therapist. They provide emotional support, and that alone sets a foundation for healing. For me, the biggest key to unlocking my healing was not only having a good well-prepared therapist, but having one who leans on the Holy Spirit in each session. I cannot stress enough the importance of having a practicing Christian faith-based therapist.

The rest is much like a safari ride—you're driving, they're guiding. Since our present struggles are often connected to past pain, you have to do some digging to find the root cause, and they guide you as you dig. They help you identify the "why" behind your thoughts, emotions, and behaviors and guide you to make healthy changes. They're able to call attention to unhealthy patterns and offer guidance on redirection.

Take me, for example. I knew I was depleted, but I was unable to pinpoint why. I knew my thoughts were not helpful, but I couldn't stop having them. Therapy helped me understand the "why" and equip me with tools to navigate my life moving forward.

Externally processing with a professional is actually a healing technique in and of itself. Their objective perspective is different from the perspective of just any outsider. They're trained to help you reframe experiences from your past and lay down any shame you carry from them. And while we're all critical of ourselves to some degree, we can reach a point where our critiques of ourselves become harsh, unhelpful, and further hinder us from healing. Your therapist can help you parse out the harsh, unhelpful criticism. Over time, you get better at being able to do this yourself.

Therapy is about learning how to heal yourself from the inside out. Because your heart, soul, mind, and strength are interlinked, your mental health influences all of them. So as you heal yourself on the inside, you begin to navigate your life on the outside in a healthier way too.

Healing Is Uncomfortable

A short time after I started therapy for postpartum depression, I picked back up with my tour dates and was traveling quite a lot again. During a radio interview with friends of mine, I was asked a super typical, run-of-the-mill question. They asked about life with a newborn and a one-year-old and how I was doing with it all. But I wasn't really prepared to be asked that.

My mind raced to figure out what to say. The true answer was definitely not going to be what they were expecting, but a false answer was going to be insincere. The truth was going to reveal more than I thought I was ready to share. A lie was going to shield me from having to be vulnerable. But I had made a promise to the Lord years before this moment that I would not lie. This question weighed heavily on me, and I had to decide how to answer in the moment. There was no "let me pray about it and get back to you" opportunity. So I decided against lying. I just wouldn't do it.

"Well, I was just diagnosed with severe postpartum depression, and I'm going through probably the darkest season of my life," I replied concisely. And then—crickets. There was a gaping silence. No words, no utterances, nothing. You could have heard a pin drop in that studio. But surprisingly, after that momentary silence, the phone lines started lighting up one right after another. People were calling in to tell me that they were going through the same thing or other mental health challenges and that they were encouraged by my confession.

I'm not encouraging you to call into a radio show to publicly share your decision to heal. But I am encouraging you to know that there is nothing shameful about having been wounded, still hurting, or needing help. Because our society tends to reward strength, promote power, seek control, and desire instant gratification, that's not a prevalent message—though it should be. The message we hear from society is: the sooner you can recover from something, the better. So when it takes us more than five minutes to bounce back, we can feel embarrassed because we're concerned we'll be considered weak or not quite resilient enough.

When we admit that we don't have it all together—to our close circle, our family, our therapist, whomever—we put ourselves in a vulnerable position. But healing *requires* vulnerability. And true, deep, meaningful healing takes time; it's a slow process. The people who care for you will support you with tenderness. Before they can do that, you must lay down your defenses of self-protection. Unlike quick fixes or surface-level coping, real healing asks us to soften—to let down our defenses, grieve what's been lost, and sit with discomfort without immediately trying to escape it.

Healing Is Ongoing

After Moses spoke the Shema to the Israelites, they left the desert and entered the Promised Land as a whole people. Though the Promised Land flowed with milk and honey, it was not heaven on Earth. The Israelites had to keep at it, even facing more challenges to go conquer the land while maintaining their status as one nation. Comparatively, you will come to a point where your being is whole. You'll find that you are able to function completely and love fully—heart, mind, soul, and strength. You will have made your way out of the desert.

But healing isn't a box you check or a line item you cross off your to-do list. It's not even necessarily a journey that comes to an immediate end. Your healing journey out of the desert will come to an end, but we are never really done healing. From the point you step out of your desert, you will have to keep at it, upkeeping and nurturing the four integral parts of your being. Healing becomes an ongoing, continual process. It becomes maintenance work on the four integral parts of your being so that you can remain whole.

When I chose the path that would lead to healing, I also chose the harder road. I didn't waltz down an easy path, frolicking and skipping along the way. Instead, I carved out my own trail and trudged through my desert and its harsh conditions. You may be walking through your own desert right now. But if you choose to heal, you will find your way out.

And the more difficult path will turn out to be the more rewarding path.

CHAPTER 6

COURAGE OVER COMFORT

In April of 2019, Netflix released a special titled, *Brené Brown: The Call to Courage*. Brené is a research professor at the University of Houston, and she has done extensive work on shame and vulnerability. In true professor style, her special is a lecture, and in it, she teaches about choosing to have courage instead of staying in comfort. Vulnerability, she says, is the birthplace of healing: "Vulnerability is not winning or losing. It's having the courage to show up and be seen when we have no control over the outcome." Vulnerability takes courage, as does feeling painful emotions, sitting in discomfort, asking for help, being authentic, going to therapy—the whole lot of it.

Just about any motivational speaker will say that if you are comfortable, you are not growing. I would also say that if we aren't being courageous, we probably aren't healing. Healing requires vulnerability, and vulnerability requires courage—so we must choose to be courageous in order to heal.

There's really no way around it.

Pulling in the Process

If you've ever heard the phrase, "Pull yourself up by your bootstraps," it's likely been in a tough situation. In American usage, it's symbolic of determination, hard work, and self-reliance. Merriam-Webster defines it "to promote or develop by initiative and effort with little or no assistance."[43] But that hasn't always been what it meant. Originally, it was a joke.

43. "Bootstraps." *Merriam-Webster.com Thesaurus*, Merriam-Webster, https://www.merriam-webster.com/dictionary/bootstraps. Accessed 20 June 2025.

The bootstraps saying originated in the nineteenth century. Its first recorded use appeared in an article published in *The Workingman's Advocate* on October 4, 1834: "It is conjectured that Mr. Murphee will now be enabled to hand himself over the Cumberland river or a barn yard fence by the straps of his boots."[44] Mr. Murphee (whoever he was) could not have literally yanked himself up by his bootstraps. When you really think about it, the act of lifting yourself off the ground by tugging on your own bootstraps is physically impossible. To have pulled that off (or, yourself up) would have been quite the miracle. The phrase was used as an absurdity.

Over time, the phrase evolved. It progressed to being used to describe someone who had done the impossible on their own account. When someone succeeded by their own merit and hard work, they were praised for "bootstrapping." This is the meaning the phrase still carries today. If you're being told to pull yourself up by your bootstraps, you're being told to do the hard work. If you're being praised for pulling up your bootstraps, you've accomplished a challenging feat with the level of determination it took.

I pulled up my bootstraps—more like, laced up my tennis shoes—a few years ago. One of the goals I set for myself after I was diagnosed with postpartum depression was to improve my physical health. I wanted to get in shape, but I didn't care about losing weight and wasn't thinking about wearing a bathing suit in the summer. I cared about being strong for my kids, for my husband, for God's service, and for the people I lead and influence.

So I started running. People seem to either love running or absolutely despise it. Call me crazy, but as much as I detest stretching my physical limits, running is something I found

44. Benjamin Zimmer. "figurative "bootstraps" (1834)," ADS-L (Listserv), August 11, 2005, message posted to Listserv.linguistlist.org, https://listserv.linguistlist.org/pipermail/ads-l/2005-August/052756.html.

freeing. I felt like I was away from the world yet grounded in it at the same time. I also felt leg pain, stiffness, out of breath, and the most horrible side cramps—especially at the start. I started slow and short, with a simple goal. I wasn't thinking about running a 5k or even a mile. I wanted to be able to say, "I'm a little healthier today than I was yesterday."

Running became a way for me to regain my physical health and practice self-discipline because I had to have the willpower to hit the pavement (or the tread) consistently. As I gained endurance and strength, I gradually increased my training regime and set my sights on running a 5k. I never really thought I could accomplish the physical goal of running 5 kilometers. Me? Run 5,000 meters? I assumed I could train as much as I wanted, but in all likelihood, that distance was probably never really going to happen all in one go under my tennis shoes.

But I decided to give it as much effort as I could. I followed a pretty strict running plan, and I tried not to miss exercises. I've learned that runners tend to be fairly disciplined by nature, which makes sense. They pretty much have to be. If you miss a few days of training, boy do you feel it the next day you run. I didn't create a restrictive diet, but I did pay careful attention to what I was eating, trying to shovel as many nutritious foods as possible. I increased my water intake and made rest a priority. It was a slow grind, but I continued pressing on.

I vividly remember the day I reached my goal. I actually surpassed it, and I definitely didn't expect to do that. But that day, I ran 3.2 miles—a distance I never thought I would accomplish. I'd been determined to give it my best effort, and I'd worked hard to get across that finish line. My literal tennis shoes had become figurative boots. I had accomplished what I thought was impossible.

The difference between our modern era's bootstrapping and mine had been the "with little or no assistance" part. I owned my responsibility in working hard and staying disciplined, but I knew I had accomplished my distance goal with the Lord's help. My running regime was not completely self-reliant; it was God-reliant too.

For me, there was a meditative aspect to running. That's what had initially drawn me to it. It became a way for me to be in God's presence, a time for me to "take delight in the Lord" (Psalm 37:4). On my outside runs, I delighted in nature and felt joy at the strength of my body. It was a time I could admire His works and celebrate His presence. Delight came first, and my desire to be healthier and more in shape followed. When I reached my goal, I was reminded that God keeps His promises: "Take delight in the Lord, and He will give you the desires of your heart" (37:4). For me, covering that distance was the fulfillment of a promise from the Lord in my life.

Healing may seem like an impossible task, much like pulling yourself up by your bootstraps. You may be trapped in nineteenth-century thinking, believing that healing is truly impossible. That requires a shift in your mindset. Though healing may appear to be an impossible task to you, it is not a journey you have to go at alone. You don't need to rely solely on yourself. It will require hard work and determination, but it is achievable when you rely on the Lord.

For all that healing requires of us, we gain so much more on the other side. But while we're in the middle of the process, it's hard to appreciate gains you have yet to receive—and easy to forget that they are coming. You will run up against some expected challenges but also some that will take you by surprise. That's all part of the process. But all of its challenges, all of the process, requires courage. And that, you can prepare for.

Preparing for the Process

When I started running, I learned the lesson of hydration the hard way. But I only had to learn it once. I made the mistake of going on a run before drinking enough water. I'd planned to run in the morning, but the day took its own course so I ended up running later in the day in the Texas heat. In my beginner-runner mind, I had hydrated well enough in the morning that I thought I should be good in the afternoon too. But when I started getting cramps in my legs, I knew I'd been wrong. I thought I'd properly prepared my body, but I'd definitely been mistaken.

As much as possible, it's important to prepare for healing—which begins with the premise of our lives. Our ultimate goal with healing is to heal the parts of us in need of healing so we become whole—to love God and love others. We carry our motivations and desires into the healing process to reach that goal with the help of Christ, who offers us water from a well that will not run dry. He tells us in the Gospel of John, "Everyone who drinks this water will be thirsty again, but whoever drinks the water I give them will never thirst. Indeed, the water I give them will become in them a spring of water welling up to eternal life" (4:13-14). He is the water for our spiritual thirst and "the bread of life" (6:35). He is the sustainer of our souls, so our healing must take place alongside Him.

As you enter into the healing process, it's imperative that your focus be on Christ. Spend time in the Word and prayer to stay rooted in truth and to commune with our Lord. This is a practice to continue throughout the process, water to replenish yourself as you go, but it begins by building that foundation first.

He is the great healer—and there is no greater blessing than that.

Releasing During the Process

In order to heal, there are certain things we have to let go—the past being one. Having gotten used to the weight of your past doesn't mean you should continue carrying it. And you cannot move forward while you're holding onto what is behind you.

To let go of the past, you must first accept the past. And to accept the past, you have to face your past. You have to own your story, name it as yours, and admit where you've been hurt. This is difficult on a lot of levels, and it may involve acknowledging you've been hurt by people you love and who love you. You may feel shame, fear, guilt, sadness, or hurt. Moving through that discomfort instead of avoiding or numbing it becomes part of that acceptance process, as does looking at how you've coped and what you still carry.

This was the hardest part for me. Accepting the past and letting go of the past. It's not easy, but it is possible. Yes, it will hurt. Yes, it will make you angry. Yes, it will frustrate you. But your pain will ease. During your healing process, go through your time of grief, sorrow, affliction—and do it at the feet of Jesus. Feel what you need to feel, and let out the emotions you need to release. Let go of the place they are holding you.

Cling to our ever-present help, our comforter the Holy Spirit, who will walk with you through your emotions as they come. Ask for the peace that surpasses understanding. Healing will come, and joy will follow.

Enduring Throughout the Process

When I'm in the middle of training and I have a good run, its because my body responds in a way that allows me to complete that day's goal. But not every run is a good run. When I have one of those days, I do my best to keep going, even if it isn't going the way I wanted.

In the early days of my training, I had a particularly bad run that still stands out in my mind. I planned to run fifteen minutes, walk for five, then run a final eight minutes. Fourteen minutes into it, I was ready to lay down right on the road. I was so winded I contemplated stopping altogether. I gave myself the five minutes to walk, but when I started the eight-minute run portion, I hit the steepest hill on this route at the four-minute mark. The shooting pains in my calves won out, so I walked up the hill and picked back up with running once I made it to the top to finish my time. My endurance level wasn't what I'd wanted it to be, and the run had definitely gone different than I'd planned.

A couple days later, I was on a similar run in the middle of a Texas-hot day. Yet again, I ended up gasping for air during my second interval. *I'm never going to make it*, I thought. *I can't keep going like this.* Then, low and behold, the sprinklers turned on in the yard I was running past. Now, sprinklers don't just turn on midday in Dallas. They come on in the morning or evening because it's so hot during the day that the water just evaporates right into the air. But here I was standing in the middle of sprinkling water streams right when I needed them, right when I was feeling defeated for not being able to keep going as I'd planned. I ran through them, twirled around in them, and drenched myself. That day, I was refreshed and able to push through.

Isaiah 43:19 reads, "Behold, I will do a new thing, now it shall spring forth; shall you not know it? I will even make a road in the wilderness and rivers in the desert" (NKJV). In the older Reina-Valera version, one of the most widely used Spanish Bible translations, the verse reads, "I will make a way in the wilderness, and rivers in the solitude." When I was on my run on this particularly hot day, no one came by asking if I wanted a lift back to my house. No one was there to encourage me to keep going. I was alone and thought my effort depended on my endurance. But those sprinklers felt like rivers God had provided for me in the desert.

There will be days during the healing process that won't go the way you want them. But when we are at our worst and just about to give up, God always does something. He makes a road in the wilderness; He gives us rivers in our solitude. You will not be alone because God will be with you. As you endure, He will not leave you. He hasn't left you, His eyes are on you, and He will refine you through this.

The process may seem too long to make, but you need only to take it one day at a time. The key is to finish each day, one at a time. The Lord will make a road for you in your desert, with rivers in your solitude.

Persisting Through the Process

In my early stages of healing after postpartum depression and anxiety and being suicidal, running became a stress management technique for me. My soul had gotten exhausted by life's traumas, but running gave me a space to rejuvenate it. Sometimes I was discouraged because I didn't have the energy I needed on my running days, or I seemed to have too much on my mind to be able to get changed and out the door. But any process takes effort to see it through to the end, and running was no exception.

My healing process brought a lot of change into my life. They were good changes that were to the benefit of my health, but it seemed like I was having to adjust my entire life. It's never easy to change what you've been used to all your life. Even if the changes are good, they're still changes. But truly, the Lord helped me—alongside my therapist and loving friends who wanted to see me thrive.

I commonly returned to the Psalms to remember how David encouraged himself, when he spoke to his soul. He knew that our willpower comes from the soul. In Psalm 103, he says, "Praise the Lord, my soul; all my inmost being, praise His holy name." David gives us many reasons for hope through descriptions of God's compassion (v. 8), His healing and redemption (vv. 2-5), and His eternal love for us (v. 17). So we praise the Lord in good times and in bad times, in sadness and joy, in riches and poverty, in abundance or lack, in difficulty or ease. And we put our hope in the Lord.

The Lord will remind you of His presence in the most challenging moments—when the burden feels heavy, when hope seems far, when rock hits bottom. Those are the moments God will show up with words of restoration and encouragement. He will always meet us, even when we feel we have nothing left to give and as though nothing left remains. He will always be faithful so we can persist.

Continuing in the Process

Life can feel like various forms of races—a marathon, sprint, 5k, 100-meter dash. Our job is to keep going on life's course, the healing process being part of that course. When the Apostle Paul reflected on his life and ministry as he neared the end of his earthly journey, he wrote to Timothy, "I have fought the good fight, I have finished the race, I have kept the faith" (2 Timothy 4:7). He had finished his race having kept his faith.

There will be days on the healing journey that you feel like you are fighting. But continue to fight. The end may seem far away. But continue moving forward. Hope may seem lost at times. But continue to reach for it. As long as we have life, we have hope. It may not feel like you're making progress in the moment, but even the smallest steps forward add up over time. Don't let the challenges keep you from reaching your goals. Resist giving up, persevere in faith, and continue through the process, even when you don't feel like it—or perhaps, especially when you don't feel like it.

Keep moving forward.

CHAPTER 7

REST, RESET, RECOVER

Sometimes, we fight what is good for us.

When we're kids, we don't want to eat vegetables and would prefer not to brush our teeth. As teenagers, we fight curfews, coming in late if even by five minutes. Once we're adults, we'll look for any excuse to avoid a routine checkup at the doctor.

Other times, we readily accept what is *not* good for us.

As children (and some of us adults), we love to eat cookies and candy. In our teenage years, we drive fast and take lots of chances. When we're adults, we overspend or live beyond our means from time to time.

These examples don't apply to everyone of course, but they introduce my point about rest. Rest is a topic that touches on both of these categories: We will fight rest (what is good for us), and we take those thousand other things (what's not good for us). Most of the time, we fight rest *so that we can* accept the one thousand other things. We take them on *in lieu of rest*. And we end up avoiding what we need in order to keep running a race that was never meant for us to run.

The book of 1 Corinthians is a letter Paul wrote to the church in Corinth, which was a diverse city during this time. Corinth had a lot going on. Similar to the Olympic Games, the Isthmian Games was a major event held near the Isthmus of Corinth, so Paul's audience would have been familiar with the races at the Games. To illustrate how the Christian life should be lived, he compares athletes in the races to Christians in their lives, saying, "Do you not know that in a race all the runners run, but only one gets the prize? Run in such a way as to get the prize. Everyone who competes in the games goes into strict training. They do it to get a crown that will not last, but we do it to get a crown that will last forever" (1 Corinthians 9:24-27).

In these verses, Paul is encouraging believers to run the spiritual race in the same way athletes run a competitive race. Just as runners in the Isthmian Games would prioritize dedication, perseverance, and discipline, so too should Christians in their walk with the Lord. But unlike the temporary rewards athletes seek, Paul points out that Christians are striving for an eternal reward — a "crown that will last forever." This is a passage meant to motivate Christians to live intentionally for God and for an everlasting crown of eternal life.

The "strict training" that the competitive athletes adhere to requires rest. This may seem counterintuitive to non-athletes, but recovery from strenuous exercise and workouts depends on sleep. Your body simply cannot recuperate if it doesn't get adequate sleep. Today's Olympic marathoners typically aim for ten hours of sleep per night. They also sleep during the day, logging anywhere from a half-hour nap to an hour-and-a-half nap. These athletes are exceptionally in tune with their bodies and know when they need more sleep to recover. Their recovery regimens must match the demands of their extreme training routines. And they are *extreme*.

Any athlete—not just the elite—will prioritize sleep to stave off injury. For marathoners, running such long distances puts a ton of physical demand and stress on their bodies, which makes them susceptible to injury. Without divulging too much detail (since we'll cover our physical beings in a later chapter), sleep allows their muscles time to repair, immune systems to stabilize, minds to focus, and hormones to regulate.

Sleep does this for *all* of us. Our bodies are awe-inspiringly wondrous in that they can repair themselves as they do. But far too often, we keep them from being able to do their incredible job—to repair, to regulate, to recover. We mistake their resiliency for invincibility, and we run on as little sleep as we can to get by. And for what? If we're honest, we're running after the "crown that will not last."

That crown refers to anything in this world. Paul's implied warning is not to settle for temporary or worldly gains. Yet we run after, chase down, and charge at what is temporary, wearing ourselves out all the while. When we exhaust ourselves for the sake of worldly gains (which is detrimental in and of itself), we aren't adhering to the "strict training" that Paul advocates. We can't run in such a way as to get the prize because we're too sleep deprived to do so—possibly injured, sick, unfocused, and unregulated too.

Sleep is a specific category of the more broad topic of rest, which God created us to need. He Himself rested after creating the Earth. Genesis says, "By the seventh day God had finished the work He had been doing; so on the seventh day He rested from all work. Then God blessed the seventh day and made it holy, because on it He rested from all the work of creating that He had done" (2:2-3). Our Lord, God of the universe, set an example for us by resting. Our bodies require rest, as does our mental health because it affects our heart, mind, soul, and strength. Rest allows every part of our whole being to function fully. Without it, our being cannot be at its best.

The Importance of Rest

"What is the fourth commandment, and when was the last time you obeyed it?"

Those were the words I was confronted with a few years ago. I was in prayer with the Lord. That day, like many before and since, I was attempting to cast my burdens upon the Lord. But my casting was really more like complaining. I was frustrated with feeling stuck and unfulfilled. At the time, I thought there were things in my life that should have happened by then, but they hadn't. Things with career, ministry, family, and just life as a whole.

As I talked to God as a little girl whining to her dad would, I heard His sweet tender voice speak to my heart with firmness. *You are stuck, because you are in sin.* I was dumbfounded. It felt like a bucket of icy water had just been poured over me. What? In *sin*? I had been doing everything possible to purify each day for God and steer clear of sin. How could this be? So I pressed in for more, and that's when the confrontation came: *What is the fourth commandment, and when was the last time you obeyed it?* I was rendered speechless in thought. Then, the realization came that I had never really kept that commandment.

The fourth of the Ten Commandments as expressed in Exodus 20:8-11 says: "Remember the Sabbath day, to keep it holy. Six days you shall labor and do all your work, but the seventh day is the Sabbath of the Lord your God. In it you shall do no work: you, nor your son, nor your daughter, nor your male servant, nor your female servant, nor your cattle, nor your stranger who is within your gates. For in six days the Lord made the heavens and the earth, the sea, and all that is in them, and rested the seventh day. Therefore the Lord blessed the Sabbath day and hallowed it."

Now, by mentioning this, I'm not attempting to push any particular doctrine or dogma. I'm just sharing with you what I learned. The word Sabbath is a transliteration of the Hebrew word *Shabbat,* and it literally means *rest.* If we interpret the Scripture with this literal meaning in it it would read: "Remember the *rest* day, to keep it holy. Six days you shall labor and do all your work, but the seventh day is the *rest* of the Lord your God. In it you shall do *no work.*" I paraphrase here: "you, nor your family, nor your employees, nor your properties or companies, nor anyone you harbor. For in six days the Lord made the heavens and the earth, the sea, and all that is in them, and rested the seventh day. Therefore the Lord blessed the *rest* day and hallowed it."

With the coming of grace in the death and resurrection of Jesus, much of the law was rendered unnecessary; Jesus already paid the ultimate sacrifice to overcome the law. However, there's one thing from the law that we can all agree has no expiration date, and it's the Ten Commandments. Or, as I like to call them, the Big Ten. Of them all, the first three, if violated, are direct sins against God. The latter six, if violated, are sins against other people. The fourth commandment, however, is the only one of the Big Ten that, if violated, is a sin against *yourself.* And if you sin against yourself enough, it breaks you from the inside. Lack of rest is not just a sin, it is a silent killer of purpose and strength. It causes your flame to dwindle and your voice to become weaker—until it is altogether silenced.

Learning to Rest

The words we have of the Israelites' story documents their growth as a whole people, including the formation of their voice. As the Israelites made their way through the desert, they exercised their voice as a nation, though not always in what we might consider the most helpful of ways. But this was all a part of the journey that would lead them through transformation to become a healed, whole nation. The Israelites cried out to and pleaded with God frequently with fear and frustration, but it was through these moments that they learned to rely on the Lord.

One of the first instances the Israelites cry out with both fear and frustration occurs a mere two months after leaving Egypt. The people are hungry, and they cry out to Moses and Aaron, saying, "If only we had died by the Lord's hand in Egypt! There we sat around pots of meat and ate all the food we wanted, but you have brought us out into this desert to starve this entire assembly to death" (Exodus 16:3). God had just saved them from their oppression by getting them out of Egypt. They had witnessed supernatural events during their saving. And here they were, wishing to go back.

In this instance, God does not reprimand the Israelites. He simply solves the problem. Moses and Aaron were the go-betweens, and the Lord tells Moses He will send manna (bread) from heaven that the Israelites should gather each day—but only enough for that *one* day: "In this way I will test them and see whether they will follow my instructions. On the sixth day they are to prepare what they bring in, and that is to be twice as much as they gather on the other days" (vv. 4-5). Moses clarifies why they are doubling up and says to them, "Tomorrow is to be a day of sabbath rest, a holy sabbath to the Lord" (v. 23). The Lord was providing food for the Israelites while also teaching them lessons about obedience, trust, and rest. They were to follow His instructions, trust that He would provide, and rest as a whole people.

On the first day, Moses warns them that no one is to keep any of the food overnight because God's instructions are to "gather enough for that day" (v. 4). But some of them didn't listen. Whether they didn't take God's instructions seriously or were afraid that God wouldn't send more food the next day, they disobeyed the Lord. They made their to-go boxes and kept the food overnight. In the morning, however, it was ruined. Lesson learned. They were to practice obedience by doing as God commanded and trust that He would do what He said He would do, which was to provide. As this goes on for the next five days, they obey and experience a fulfillment of God's promise to them. They learn to depend upon God's provisions. They practice obedience. God keeps His promise.

When they make it to the sixth day, they gather double their regular amount so they can rest the following day. On the seventh day, Moses reminds them why they gathered twice as much of a normal day's portion on the sixth day: "You will not find any of it on the ground today. Six days you are to gather it, but on the seventh day, the Sabbath (rest day), there will not be any" (vv. 24-26). Again, some of the Israelites don't listen and head out to gather their food just like the six days before—but Scripture says that "they found none" (v. 27). This was a misstep for two reasons. First, God had given them clear instructions not to gather food. Second, he'd told them to rest. Whether they didn't believe there wouldn't be food or they didn't see the point of resting, they disobeyed the Lord.

God reiterates His prioritization of rest to the Israelites, saying, "Bear in mind that the Lord has given you the Sabbath; that is why on the sixth day He gives you bread for two days. Everyone is to stay where they are on the seventh day; no one is to go out" (v. 29). It took the Israelites being told a few times—and a few trial and error runs for some of them—but they came to understand that rest was of great importance to the Lord: "So the people rested on the seventh day" (v. 30). Reading this portion sets off an applause soundtrack in my brain. Way to go to the people of Israel for finally trusting God to provide!

This lesson of obedience, trust, and rest was foundational in the Israelites' journey. They had a long way to go before becoming a whole people ready to enter the Promised Land, but this was a formative experience for them. When they disobeyed, God redirected them and remained with them as they reoriented their thinking. They learned to trust that God would provide for them and guide them on their journey.

The same chapter in Exodus that begins with their cry to the Lord and documents their lesson of rest ends with a beautiful spoiler: "The Israelites ate manna forty years, until they came to a land that was settled; they ate manna until they reached the border of Canaan" (v. 35). This verse tells us two things: the Israelites continued to practice obedience to the Lord, and God provided food to them for as long as they needed—which was the entirety of their desert season.

Be it rather disrespectfully, they had practiced using their voice, crying out to God in their distress. But even though their cry was not perfectly formed, God did not hesitate to provide for them. They cried out, and God answered their cry. There are times I look back at and wish I would have been more respectful in some of my cries to the Lord. But He has been so loving and kind to graciously hear my cries no matter how they've come to Him. He has provided for me time and time again, fulfilling promises over me in His loving kindness. The Lord will do the same for you in your healing journey. Open your heart and cry out to Him in your distress. Practice obedience to Him, coming to Him with each new day and each new step. He is worthy of our trust, and He will provide for you as you choose to journey courageously on your way to healing.

Resetting Our System

God is serious about rest—so serious that He made it a commandment for the Israelites and arranged their food-gathering initiative around it. He prioritized rest for them, teaching them to rest so that they would learn the practice of rest for themselves. He knew they needed to rest to function at their full capacity—heart, soul, mind, and body. Like theirs, our bodies require a certain amount of rest, and we can only go so long without it. When we are healthy, we must maintain a scheduled rest cycle to remain healthy. When we are healing, our bodies naturally require more than usual.

We all have our own daily patterns and ways of doing things that we naturally create for our life-rhythms. When we create unhealthy life-rhythms, we adapt to those patterns in unhealthy ways that affect our heart, soul, mind, and strength—our whole being. So your "normal" amount of rest may not be up to par. In other words, you may not be resting as much as you should be—or resting as God intends. So you have to reset your system a bit, especially as you enter into healing. It's important we create a solid foundation of rest for us to maintain both during the initial healing process and after in maintenance healing.

To reset our system (both our bodies and life rhythms), we must realign ourselves with the rhythm God intends for us, which includes resting *with* God. To see what this looks like, we need not look any further than Jesus to have a guide by which to model ourselves after. He did this regularly—in the morning, around major events, and in times of sorrow or stress.

Rest to Prepare

The first recorded instance of Jesus spiritually resting with God in solitude takes place right after His baptism before the beginning of His public ministry.[45] Though they are not detailed, this would not have been the first instance that Jesus rested spiritually with the Lord. He would have developed restful life patterns, participating in Sabbath rest and daily rhythms throughout His life. After His baptism, Jesus is led by the Spirit into the wilderness for forty days and nights to be alone with God—not to rest in a physical sense, but in a spiritual one.

Jesus intentionally withdraws to the wilderness not just to prepare for ministry but to commune deeply with the Father. This wilderness, known as the Judean Wilderness, is a desert-like region that stretches between Jerusalem and the Dead Sea. It is a dry, rocky, and rugged land. Though there are a plethora of cliffs, ravines, hills, and the occasional cave, the Judean Wilderness has little vegetation or shade. The days are hot, and the nights are cold. It doesn't rain much, and wild animals roam around the terrain.

Sound familiar? The wilderness Jesus entered was not the same desert where the Israelites wandered for forty years, though the two are connected both geographically and theologically. The desert, both for Jesus and the Israelites, was a place that represented spiritual formation and preparation. It is a place stripped of comfort, where dependence on God is vital. In a place of solitude

45. Matthew 4:1–11; Mark 1:12–13;. Luke 4:1–13

and weakness, Jesus aligns Himself with God's will, resisting temptation and grounding His identity in the Lord's love before embarking on a new phase of life. This was a time of sacred rest and intimacy with God.

A Prayer for Preparation

Lord,
As I prepare to enter into a season of healing, prepare the way ahead for me. Though I am still in the desert, I know you are in the desert with me. I know I will feel uncomfortable, afraid, and even hurt as I engage in this process, but I know you will be with me as I do. I desire to prepare with you for the journey. And, please, teach me how to rest.
Amen.

Rest to Refocus

After Jesus begins His public ministry, it very quickly gains momentum. Despite the pressing needs around Him and His growing popularity, He prioritizes time alone with God. Jesus knew His strength and clarity came from time with God, especially amid days filled with demands and crowds. The Gospel of Mark describes Jesus seeking solitude and rest with the Lord after a long evening: "Very early in the morning, while it was still dark, Jesus got up, left the house and went off to a solitary place, where He prayed" (Mark 1:35). He makes rising early to seek the Lord a priority—not retroactively but proactively.

A Prayer for Refocusing

Lord,
My life is full of tasks I cannot accomplish and needs I am unable to meet. I am weighed down by the demands of life, but I know that time spent with you will bear fruit far more rewarding than any of this world. Open my eyes to see the evidence of your work in my life so that I remember your presence as you go with me. Give me strength for my days and clarity for seeing you in them.
Amen.

Rest to Discern

Midway into His ministry, it came time for Jesus to choose His core disciples. He'd spent time ministering and now needed the disciples who would become key leaders in the early church. The night before Jesus chose the Twelve, He "went out to a mountainside to pray, and spent the night praying to God" (Luke 6:12). Again, He retreats to be alone with the Lord. Before making a critical decision, Jesus spends the entire night in prayer on a mountain. He knew discernment and direction required time in God's presence.

A Prayer for Discernment

Lord,
Each day of healing presents challenges, difficulties, and decisions, and I ask for your guidance as I navigate through the process. With my eyes focused on you, I seek to follow you. Show me your ways as I navigate my path, and make it clear before me. Lead and direct me as I walk closely with you in every moment.
Amen.

Rest to Restore

When Jesus learns of John the Baptist's death, His first course of action is to retreat for rest with God. But the crowds follow Him, and "he had compassion on them and healed their sick" (v. 14). The disciples suggest Jesus dismiss them to find food and eat. Instead, Jesus feeds them Himself—from five loaves of bread and two fish (v. 17). This was no small group or even several small groups put together. There were "five thousand men, besides women and children" (v. 21), yet they had twelve baskets full of leftovers. Jesus had done miraculous work in the midst of His grief. He would have been exhausted in every way. So, after they left, Jesus "went up on the mountainside by Himself to pray" (v. 23). Time and time again Jesus returns to a place of solitude to commune with the Lord to be restored emotionally, mentally, physically, and spiritually.

A Prayer for Restoration

Lord,
When my heart and soul are downcast, lift them up so I may continue on my journey. As I seek you in solitude, keep me from attempting to escape the difficulties of healing so that I may, instead, engage with its challenges. Reveal to me a rhythm of life that honors you and brings healing to my being through intentional rest.
Amen.

In all these instances, Jesus models how rest in God leads to clarity and purpose. In each of these moments—before ministry, amid busyness, in grief, and before decision-making—Jesus shows that rest with God isn't optional. Rest allowed Him to prepare, refocus, discern, and restore.

As followers of Jesus, we are to look to His example to know how to build our life's patterns. These moments of rest create a clear outline for how we can reset our system, dissolving unhealthy patterns for life-giving practices.

Resting *with* the Lord gives us the ability to heal.

PART III

A VOICE TO PREPARE THE WAY —THROUGH THE DESERT

PREPARATION

CHAPTER 8

READY THE WAY FOR THE LORD

So far, we have covered a lot of ground.

Let's take it back to *our* beginning (chapter one of this book) and *the* beginning (chapter one of the Bible). The first verse in the Bible reads, "In the beginning God created the heavens and the earth" (1:1). The very first verse of the Bible establishes God as the Creator of everything. Twenty-six verses later, God creates man: "So God created mankind in His own image, in the image of God He created them; male and female He created them" (v. 27). This is one of the most foundational verses in the Bible regarding human identity and purpose. It tells us that all people bear the image of God, the creator of all things. There is one God who created life with purpose and meaning, and He is worthy of all glory.

As human beings made in His image, we are designed to reflect His character, live in loving relationship with Him, and align our lives with His will. We are to reflect His glory in all we do because human life has a divine origin *and* purpose. God desires a relationship with us and sent Jesus for us, as the Gospel of John records: "For God so loved the world that He gave His one and only Son, that whoever believes in Him shall not perish but have eternal life" (3:16). From that, we can explore what flows from that love—our purpose. We are to glorify God, live according to His will, and love others as a natural outflow of our love for Him. This is our highest calling, our purpose.

But you can't really have a purpose without some kind of a premise to work from. Put another way, the premise sets the stage, while the purpose guides the direction because a clear premise supports the achievement of a clear purpose. The premise is the foundational idea that supports the purpose. This brings us back to our beginning in chapter one, the premise of our lives: "Love the Lord your God with all your heart and with all your soul and with all your mind and with all your strength… Love your neighbor as yourself" (Mark 12:30). With this as our premise, we are starting with the idea that loving God is the foundation of life. We are meant to live in relationship with God, reflect His love to others, and fulfill His will on Earth.

Our premise is the rooted love for God. Our purpose is the life that love produces. We can only step fully into our purpose when our premise is rooted, clear, and firmly grounded. If the premise is flawed, incomplete, or broken, then the actions flowing from it (our purpose) will be misguided or ineffective. It's like building a house on shaky ground: no matter how well you build the house, the structure won't stand strong on an unstable foundation. Only when our foundation is healed and anchored in truth can we confidently move forward and bear the fruit of our calling.

We can move fully into the purpose of our lives when we are whole, healed beings—heart, soul, mind, and strength. When we live from a place of restoration, we reflect God's image more clearly and love others more freely. Keeping this end goal at the forefront of our minds is the key to being able to press on, to endure, to persist in the healing process. That means we must expectantly watch and prepare for the Lord in the midst of it all.

Now, let's get back to our desert.

I've described what being in a figurative desert is like. If not in this moment, you have likely resonated with those descriptions at some point. We've addressed the discovery work we have to do from within the desert—both realizing and accepting our situation. We've discussed the formative experience this season can be, learning to depend on God while inside the desert. So now, how do we begin making our way *through* the desert?

We begin in worship, right alongside the Word.

Worship and the Word

God created life with purpose and meaning (Genesis 1:27), and Jesus gave us a roadmap to get to that meaning and purpose (Mark 12:30). We know this from Scripture—God's Word. It is our compass to navigate through life's ups and downs—including the healing process. When we cannot find a safe place to rest, we can use his. When we struggle along our way, feeling as though we lack direction or guidance, God's Word guides and leads us. It is God's Word that gives us the foundation of our belief that he, as creator of the universe, is worthy of all praise, glory, and honor. When we return to it, we are reminded over and over again of God's greatness, which naturally compels us to worship.

Having been a worship leader for over two decades, I've worshipped in and through many states—one of those states being brokenness. And worshipping in a broken state is hard.

Grievers, for example, will tell you this. In grief, emotions are raw and painful. Grievers often feel as though they're sitting right on the edge of tipping into tears at every moment, with their emotions just under the surface of their skin. But in grief, brokenhearted in our suffering, worship can foster a deep longing for the Lord's comfort. It is natural for worship to stir our emotions because it brings us closer to God's presence.

I've often described depression as feeling like I'm walking with a constant dark cloud over my head. Life doesn't feel as vibrant as I once knew, and I don't feel as alive in it. Everything just generally seems dim and unappealing, sometimes even worship.

But I have learned that seeking God's presence in worship is a balm to our soul, an aid to healing its hurt. Yes, the heaviness of life has a way of weighing down our shoulders. In those moments, I must still choose to remember that, despite our circumstances, God is still good. And because He remains good, I sacrifice praise to Him, despite how we feel. Time has shown me that worship invigorates your strength and brings progress to the healing process.

We are more apt to offer our praise as a response to His greatness. The more we seek to be reminded of His goodness, the more we will be—every single time. In worship, we encounter God's greatness, recognizing His love, mercy, and power. We remember His work through songs, prayers, and Scripture that recall His faithfulness and promises. And we experience the Holy Spirit move in our hearts and deepen our faith. It engages our mind and heart in a close relationship with God, healing our souls and invigorating our strength.

In Spirit and in Truth

Let's cover a quick Sunday school lesson.

The Holy Spirit is the third person of the Trinity—fully God, co-equal with the Father and the Son (Matthew 28:19). The Holy Spirit is often described as a person, but not in the physical-body or human-being way. The Spirit possesses qualities of personhood—intellect, will, emotion, relationship—and isn't some abstract force or removed entity. The Spirit teaches (John 14:26), perceives (1 Corinthians 2:10-11), distributes spiritual gifts (1 Corinthians 12:11), feels (Ephesians 4:30), leads (Romans 8:26), and speaks (Acts 13:2).

The Spirit is God's active presence in the world and within believers, guiding, empowering, comforting, and convicting.

Throughout Scripture, the Holy Spirit is portrayed as the one who gives life (Genesis 2:7), reveals truth (John 16:13), and transforms hearts (Ezekiel 36:26-27). The Spirit continues speaking and leading today, dwelling within those who follow Christ. He equips us with spiritual gifts, produces fruit like love, joy, peace, and gives us the strength to live out God's will. John 14:26 calls the Spirit "the Advocate" who God sent when Jesus died to teach and remind us of all that Jesus said during His time on Earth. The Spirit's role is personal and His presence relational—God with us and in us (Romans 8:11).

When Jesus came, so did a new era of worship. He opened the doors for anyone from anywhere to know and worship God. He laid the foundation for worship as personal, spiritual, and truth-centered: "Yet a time is coming and has now come when the true worshipers will worship the Father in the Spirit and in truth, for they are the kind of worshipers the Father seeks. God is spirit, and His worshipers must worship in the Spirit and in truth" (John 4:23-24). In this passage, Jesus is speaking to a Samaritan woman at Jacob's well. Knowing Jesus is Jewish and she is Samaritan, she brings up a long-time issue between the two ethnicities: worship.

Let's preemptively address a few potential points of confusion. First, the "time" Jesus is referring to is the new era of worship that has come with Him and will come to fruition at the time of His resurrection, when God will send the Holy Spirit. This new time is marked by worship in Spirit and in truth—a worship that's empowered by the Holy Spirit and grounded in the truth of Christ. Next, "spirit" is lowercase in "God is spirit" and capitalized in two instances: "worship in the Spirit." The first refers to God's essence. He is invisible, eternal, not bound by space or time—he is spiritual. The two other instances refer to the Holy Spirit, who empowers and enables true worship. Worshiping "in the Spirit" means worship that is led, inspired, and made possible by the Holy Spirit.

Worship location was part of the conflict between Jews and Samaritans.[46] She doesn't flat out ask, "Where are we supposed to worship?" But she does bring it up. Jesus shifts the focus away from *where* to *how* and *who*. He mentions "the true worshipers" and "the kind of worshipers the Father seeks."

They worship "in the Spirit." Their worship is from their full *essence*. It is driven to action from the very breath that makes us who we are. It is led by the Holy Spirit, authentically derived from the heart. It is not limited to specific moments of worship, but it is an ongoing lifestyle of worship that aligns our essence (Spirit) with His essence (Spirit).

They worship "in truth." Their worship is *Godly* and *sound*, based on Scripture and aligned with believing Jesus is "the Way, the Truth, and the Life" (John 14:6). But also, their worship is *honest*. It is a pursuit of God, regardless of our circumstances. It is saying to Him, "This is me, all of me—the good, the bad, and the in-betweens. I'm not perfect, but You are. You are always worthy of my worship."

Jesus explains the kind of worshipers God wants us to be: those who worship "in the Spirit and in truth." This kind of worship calls for a whole-person response to God—authentic and grounded, not manufactured or performative. He doesn't want an outward performance; rather, He desires inward sincerity. But how do we worship honestly without letting human opinions or raw emotion define the experience?

---

46. The religious and ethnic divide between Jews and Samaritans had been going on for over 700 years by the time of Jesus' encounter with the Samaritan woman in John 4. The Jews were taught that worship was to take place in the template, and the Samaritans believed it was to be on Mount Gerizim. For more on this divide, see 2 Kings 17 (the Assyrian conquest and the origins of the Samaritan people) and Ezra 4:1–5 (the Jewish resistance to Samaritan involvement in rebuilding the temple).

Think about the "my truth" saying that's taken society by storm, especially on social media, in recent years. At its most basic level, "my truth" means "my personal experience or perspective." In today's lingo, it's about how someone feels or what they've experienced in life. But "my truth" may be emotionally real yet not factually true.

Take, for example, a girl who calls her boyfriend after leaving a job interview. But he doesn't answer the phone. She's immediately disappointed and hurt. He doesn't really care how my interview went, she thinks. That's why he's intentionally ignoring my call. She's sure this is true. He always has his phone with him, so he's obviously screened her call. There's just no other reason he wouldn't answer. But the facts? As it turns out, her boyfriend had gone to the restroom and left his phone on the table. Upon seeing her missed call, he jumps up to call her back. He's just as excited to hear about her interview as she is to tell him.

This is a relatively harmless, somewhat silly example. But it's a clear illustration of how someone's "truth" can be emotionally real but not based on factual truth. Her truth, as our culture would call it, is shaped by emotions of disappointment and hurt. The truth is based on a verifiable fact—a reason for the ignored call. Culture should have called this "my realness," which would have alleviated a lot of confusion. Or just called it what it is: subjective truth. Real emotions are central to subjective truth—and they often create it. Here's how it works: You experience a feeling. Your brain tries to make sense of that feeling. It comes up with a belief. That belief becomes "your truth."

We start to approach the danger zone when we lose sight of *the* truth and use our feelings to shape or construct *our* truth. As relatively harmless as "my truth" might have started, it's morphed into meaning something more along the lines of "a belief that someone considers truth because it feels real, even if others don't see it that way." Or worse, "even when it can be proven otherwise." There are so many issues that can stem from this.

Back to our example. Imagine the boyfriend had no idea she was going to call as soon as she did. Right when he saw the missed call, he was eager to respond and hear about her interview. In allegiance to her "truth," the girl stands firm, believing he ignored her on purpose. Her mind has filled in the blanks: He always has his phone. He didn't answer. He must not care. She can't be convinced otherwise.

At this point, things get dangerously dicey. We don't need to psychoanalyze their relationship to see how this can go downhill—and fast. It's one thing for the girlfriend to say she felt hurt when he didn't answer. Our emotions themselves are always valid; they're real physiological and psychological responses. It's another to hold fast to the emotions-based narrative that she has self-created. Did she really feel hurt? Yes, that was a real feeling she experienced. But did he really ignore her? No, that's not true. The story we attach to the emotion is not always accurate.

As Christians choosing to heal, we feel what we feel. They are real experiences that only we personally know. As part of our healing process, we must allow our emotions to pass through us, refusing to numb, avoid, or suppress them. But we cannot allow them to inform us about what is and is not true. Our emotions are *real*, but they are not the truth. Our truth is anchored in God's nature and Word, not in an internal experience.

It is with this mindset that we should approach worship. Honest worship means you come to God as you truly are—joyful or grieving, strong or weak, happy or angry—while still acknowledging His unchanging nature, regardless of our circumstances. It means you don't perform or hide, but you do remain grounded in who is, not how we feel alone. This is why God's Word must be our foundation—so we remain grounded in the truth of His character. Psalm 62:8 says, "Pour out your hearts to Him, for God is our refuge." We bring our emotions—sadness, anger, hurt—with us, *and* remember who He is.

We don't have to hide our feelings from the Lord. He gave us emotions, and He knows the ones we are feeling. But emotions are to be expressed, not followed blindly. We bring our joy, pain, or numbness to God—but we respond to truth, not just to how we feel in the moment. Emotions are expressions, but they are not a solid source of truth. Your true worship may involve tears or silence, and that is perfectly acceptable to the Lord. But it should remain rooted in who God is—not only how we feel. So we have to keep our understanding of God anchored in Scripture. And that means we have to be careful of popular culture or opinions. Our worship is not just about style or music or setting—and I say this as someone who's been a worship leader for most of my life.

Regularly being in God's Word will inform your worship. Allowing the Holy Spirit to lead you in worship will help steer you away from following trends or dangerous emotions. And sometimes, speaking or singing what is true about God, even if your feelings don't match your words yet, is a good place to start.

Jesus' outline of how we are to worship should be of great comfort to us on our healing journey. Jesus also reminds us that "God is spirit," meaning He is everywhere at all times and our worship to Him is not limited to a specific time nor a particular place. God meets us in every season, in any location—the desert included. After all, Jesus' conversation with the Samaritan woman began with a simple request for water, a request that someone in a desert might make.

Preparing with Worship

In Numbers 21, the Israelites are traveling through the desert, coming from a previous stop at a place called Mattanah: "From there they continued on to Beer, the well where the Lord said to Moses, 'Gather the people together and I will give them water.'" (Numbers 21:16). When God provides water for them, they spontaneously break out in song and praise God for the well he's provided. They become one voice, worshipping in the middle of their journey through the wilderness:

Spring up, O well!
Sing about it,
about the well that the princes dug,
that the nobles of the people sank—
the nobles with scepters and staffs.

With the Song of the Well, the Israelites use their voices in worship as they move through the desert. This passage illustrates to us that God provides for us in desert seasons, and we can respond with gratitude and song, in praise and worship. This became part of the Israelites story, and it was a mile marker of their maturing faith.

Our worship is part of how we prepare the way for the Lord as we journey through the desert. With the desert as a place where we can learn to depend on God, it is also a period when we can prepare spiritually—a season of transformation. While you are progressing through the desert, you are adding to your story. Specifically, you are adding a healing season, a process in which you are becoming whole. As you heal, you are creating your story while simultaneously preparing to tell your story.

Your story, your testimony of what God has done and is doing in your life, is yours to tell. Sharing it is a form of worship, of bringing glory to God. God has been worthy of all praise since the beginning, as creator of all things and of mankind in His image. Spoiler alert: He will be worthy through the end for the same, just as the very last book of the Bible foretells: "You are worthy, our Lord and God, to receive glory and honor and power, for you created all things, and by your will they were created and have their being" (Revelation 4:11).

CHAPTER 9

EXPECT FREEDOM AND TRAIN EXPECTANTLY

"So if the Son sets you free, you will be free indeed" (John 8:36). Jesus speaks these words during a confrontation with religious leaders who prided themselves on their lineage and law-keeping. As descendants of Abraham, they believed they were already free—and claimed to be so. But Jesus challenged that assumption, teaching that true freedom isn't found in heritage or outward obedience. True freedom, Jesus says, is found in knowing and abiding in Him.

Freedom is found in Jesus. It's available to us through a relationship with Him, one that's rooted in trust and truth. Our relationship with Jesus is one of reciprocity: when we offer ourselves to Him—through focus, surrender, faith—he meets us, shapes us, and draws us deeper into freedom. It's not transactional, but it is interactive and dynamic. It's a relationship where our action invites a response, and that response changes us.

When it comes to freedom, pain can just flat out get in the way. Pain and freedom aren't necessarily antonyms, but if they were sports teams, they'd definitely be rivals. You wouldn't find one holding an afternoon practice in the other's arena. The same is true when it comes to healing—in that the two don't always play well together.

Pain can distract us from Jesus. Instead of focusing on him, we're tempted to fixate on our pain, which moves us further from the freedom He offers. To be clear, this is not a reason to avoid pain. We've already established that acknowledging painful emotions has to be part of the healing process. But it is the reason to focus on Jesus. Keeping our eyes fixed on Him is the only way we come to experience freedom—because He is the one who makes freedom possible.

In the midst of suffering, freedom can feel like a far-fetched idea—something distant and unreachable—because pain has a sneaky way of distorting our ability to envision the future. Depending on its intensity, pain can make even the concept of a future seem impossible to grasp. That's often why we instinctively turn to immediate relief. It's why we'll reach for anything that might dull the ache in the moment. For those caught in the throes of depression or trapped in a long-term, anxiety-ridden state, the idea of freedom may seem not only unlikely, but completely out of reach.

But the point of feeling pain is to release it. When we release pain from the past during the healing process, we create space to focus on Jesus. Then, as we focus on Him, we move further from that pain with clarity. As we experience pain in the present, focusing on Jesus helps us move through it with strength. By turning our eyes to Jesus, we can more clearly see the freedom that comes with healing. I would go so far as to argue that the more impossible freedom seems, that's all the more reason to choose to heal and focus on Christ.

To do this, we must help ourselves *be able* to focus—creating space mentally, emotionally, and spiritually—so we can truly receive what Jesus is offering. Freedom in Christ is real, and we should expect the freedom Jesus promises. But we have to clear the way to live in it.

"It's Friday, and the body knows."

In 2021, I was training for my first 5k race. When you're a beginner runner training for a race, you do a lot of thinking about your body—at least, this was the case for me. When I'd go out for a run, I was constantly thinking about how my body was operating—but involuntarily so.

At first, I wasn't really setting out to consciously think about what was going on with my body. Those thoughts were coming all on their own. On those initial runs, I would return home defeated by how hard the training felt. My common thoughts on a run were, *I can't breathe. I need water. I'm in pain.* Later, in my determination to reach my goal, I came across a fact about the thought-body relationship. A neuroscientist named Candace Pert discovered that negative thought actually weakens your muscles! The body responds to thought stimuli with something that she calls "informational substances" (hormones and chemicals) that are generated with thought.[47] With my negative thinking, I was literally setting up my body for failure.

After learning this vital information, I had to make adjustments to my mindset if I wanted to succeed. With each day of training, I dedicated myself to learn more about my body and what I needed to be paying attention to. All while making sure to keep my mind positive. I started doing little check-ins with my body along the way, asking myself, "Am I pushing too hard on this run? Do I feel any signs of dehydration? Am I landing lightly and midfoot? Along with thinking, I've got this. I know I can do it. I am fearfully and wonderfully made. God has equipped me to be able to handle this." These became intentional thoughts that helped me do physical self-checks. I became quite fascinated with how my body adapted and what it was capable of.

I started to appreciate all the times I *wasn't* having to ask myself these questions or say my internal pep talks. Our bodies have the ability and intelligence to keep us alive in dire circumstances

---

47. Pert, Candace B., Michael R. Ruff, Richard J. Weber, and Miles Herkenham. 1985. "Neuropeptides and Their Receptors: A Psychosomatic Network." The Journal of Immunology 135 (2): 820–26.

but also in everyday life. We don't have to tell ourselves to breathe or instruct our hearts to beat. We don't have to set timers reminding ourselves we need water or a thermometer to regulate our body temperature. When we need water, we're thirsty. When we're hot, we sweat. God created our bodies to be able to naturally take care of themselves.

Years before I started running, I'd heard about this built-in intelligence of the body in the country I grew up in. Puerto Rico's culture is one that embraces celebrations. No one loves a fun time more than a Puerto Rican. There's a popular saying in Puerto Rico that falls right in line with its celebratory culture: "It's Friday, and the body knows." The idea is that you're drained by the end of the workweek. You've logged your hours at work, and you're ready to unwind and celebrate. When Friday rolls around, you're ready to start the weekend, enjoy your time off, and get together with your friends and family. But the phrase hits on something beyond Puerto Rico's culture: "the body knows" is a reminder of just how much the body knows—beyond what our mind realizes.

Survive. That's the body's mission. As fun as the Puerto Rican phrase is, it carries a serious underlying truth. In its mission to stay alive, the body stores stress and trauma. Clinical psychologist Dr. Nicole LePera describes this as your body's way of helping because it "isn't sabotaging you. It's protecting you."[48] Her research is a blend of psychology and holistic principles—and she is a big believer in healing yourself. She has brought recognition to the saying, "The body keeps score," which she describes as meaning "that when we experience complex trauma, it's our body that's physically changed."[49] We carry trauma that's happened to us

48. Lepera, Nicole. *How to Do the Work: Recognize Your Patterns, Heal from Your Past, and Create Your Self*, 2021.

49. Dr. LePera's research has also drawn attention to a book by Bessel Van der Kolk titled, *The Body Keeps the Score: Brain, Mind, and Body in the Healing of Trauma* (published by Penguin Books in 2015).

along with us, often unbeknownst to our mind. Our mind may stop thinking about it. But our body? It's "always trying to protect us by staying in a heightened, threatened state."[50]

Our body reacts automatically to physical sensations and emotional prompts. When you accidentally place your finger on a pan that just came out of the oven, you immediately jerk your hand back. When you watch a hilarious comedy scene in a movie, you smile and laugh hysterically. The same holds true with all that our bodies are keeping score of, especially stress and trauma. Our bodies react automatically in the same way. When you smell a scent that reminds you of a traumatic time in your life, your body may immediately tense. When you visit a house where something terrible happened to you, your body may pump adrenaline sending you signs of anxiety. After trauma, our system can stay stuck in survival mode, repeating these reactions even when we're safe. This is all part of the body's score-keeping system.

I wasn't aware of my body's ability to remember—especially with my mind being able to forget—until I started healing. Then, I became keenly aware of just how meticulous of a score my body had been keeping—for years. Through studying about mental health, I realized my body had been racking up memories of traumatic, hurtful, and stressful situations all my life. And I hadn't completely healed its pain. Certain smells, places, and even sensations would cause tension or anxiety, but I hadn't made the connection between my past stress and trauma and my body's real-time reaction. In an attempt to protect itself, my body had held onto painful memories and "kept a score."

Real healing happens when your heart, soul, mind, and body are all part of the process—especially when trauma is involved.

---

50. @the.holistic.psychologist. "The body keeps score." *Instagram*, November 1, 2023. https://www.instagram.com/reel/CzHa-DoyhAL/?hl=en.

As you start the healing process, you may think similar to the way I did when I started running. You're aware you feel stress, sense when you become tense, or recognize the sensation of building anxiety. These are messages that your body is sending you. Just as I did as I progressed through my training, start to learn about your body, turning your thoughts to healing the cause of its adverse reactions. If you can't sleep, become overwhelmed, or feel disconnected, pay attention. Your body is remembering, and it's time to pay attention to it.

God, in His infinite mercy, gave you an intelligent body. It is the vessel He gave us within which to dwell. Listen to it. Pay attention to it. And honor it by giving it the care it deserves.

Practicing Spiritual Disciplines

When I first decided to run a 5k, it took discipline to train so that I would be able to run that race. I had to run on my planned-run days to be able to keep running farther distances. As my training went on, my endurance levels increased where I could run continuously for longer distances. Spiritual discipline and endurance work the same way. We know that it is through Jesus alone that we are able to experience freedom, and He promises us that freedom. Because pain can distract us from Jesus, we have to be all the more equipped to remain focused on Him. That requires training. And it is spiritual discipline that develops the endurance we need to stay focused on Jesus.

I have grown to love the spiritual discipline of meditating for what it's taught me about being in the presence of the Lord. Meditation has become a place of stillness where I can hear God more clearly and let His truth settle deep in my heart. It's a special time that I can connect to God. I meditate on runs, training my mind to focus on Him and quiet the distractions. I've also learned to expect that I sense God's freedom during meditation as well—freedom from anxiety, fear, and striving. Interlinked with healing, meditation has become part of my spiritual training.

The word "meditation" carries several different connotations and appears in lots of different contexts. In modern day, it's a mental practice meant to eliminate distractions and improve focus, with a goal of mental clarity, emotional serenity, and physical relaxation. The biblical definition of meditation—and yes, there is a biblical definition—differs from secular definitions. The only meditation I practice and recommend is Biblical meditation. It is a practice of deep, prayerful reflection on God's Word and His character, with a goal of spiritual intimacy. Instead of thinking about meditation as a time to empty your mind, think about it as a time to fill your whole being with God's Word.

Personally, I don't have a strict or formal process for it. To me, meditating should be enjoyable, a time to relax—not an obligation with a specific workflow sequence. I put on some calm, soothing music—something I could have playing while I'm reading or sleeping. I begin by thinking about the premise of my life, of all our lives: "Love the Lord your God with all your heart and with all your soul and with all your mind and with all your strength." In those first few moments, I try to align my whole being to focus on the Holy Spirit, my friend and comforter.

To prepare, I take several deep breaths, releasing the tension in my body as I exhale slowly with each one. I feel my heartbeat slow as my heartrate calms, and I let go of the adrenaline coursing through my body. It is a time to fully embody Psalm 46:10, to "be still and know" that He is God.

Then, I try to become aware of what's going on in my heart. What strong emotions am I feeling? Am I feeling more than one? God cares about all our emotions. Glad or sad, comfortable or uncomfortable, positive or negative. I consider if there's one that's overriding the rest. What is it? Do I feel calm? Am I feeling fulfilled? Empowered? Weak? I check in with my heart first.

Next, I'll turn my attention to my soul, asking myself what my motivations are. Am I aligned with what God wants for me? Am I chasing anything that is of my desire or of pleasures in this life? Do I want to be moved by the Holy Spirit, or am I trying to stifle the Spirit's presence? Am I allowing my will to take precedence over the Lord's will for my life?

Last, I end in prayer to connect with God, staying in tune with my spirit. I use this time to worship, lifting up praise to the Lord. I express my gratitude for His holiness, my thankfulness for His blessings, and my adoration of who He is. I use this time to recenter my focus on who God is. I'll usually end by playing worship music (if I hadn't already been playing some already).

Meditation is time to consider, reflect on, and check in with your whole being—heart, soul, mind, body. When I can breathe deeply, feeling as though a weight has been lifted off my shoulders, I fall into step with the Holy Spirit and carry that peace with me throughout the day. No matter what problems will come up later in the day and no matter what problems I may have already faced earlier, I feel the presence of the Lord in these moments of meditation. I know He is with me, and I have peace that drives out fear. When I feel that peace, I've completed my meditation.

Some people meditate for 15 minutes, an hour, or even two or three hours a day. Everyone's meditation practices look different. It all depends on what you need. I don't always have time to meditate in the early morning, and I don't want to feel rushed or have to hurry through it. So each morning, I look at the schedule for my day ahead and find several slots throughout the day where I will have time—that way, I stay disciplined, learning and growing in my intimate relationship with the Lord. And when I start to feel tense or dysregulated, I ask myself, have I meditated on God's Word today? Usually, the answer to that question in moments of stress is either no or not enough.

The most important thing is to be able to align your being so that your whole self can praise the Lord with each breath you take.

Developing Spiritual Endurance

Implementing spiritual disciplines in our lives increases our spiritual endurance—our ability to remain focused on Jesus and the freedom He offers us. The Bible tells us to keep God's Word constantly in our thoughts and actions because it shapes every part of our being and our lives. This means one of our spiritual practices must be going to His Word.

The Word of God is not merely words for our intellect to process. It is God's living breath translated to words that we can understand. It is *alive* and actively speaks to the innermost depths of our being (Hebrews 4:12). It is also our daily bread that feeds the life within us (Matthew 4:4). As daily cooked meals bring nourishment to our bodies, so does the Word of God—the Bread of Life—bring nourishment to our spirit, the part of our being that connects us to God.

I use an easy-to-remember practice for spiritual training called the 10-10-10 model. At its most basic level, you spend ten minutes in worship, ten minutes in the Word, and ten minutes in prayer. Sometimes, I spend ten minutes worshipping the Lord, and then ten minutes in prayer, making petitions, supplications, and pleas to the Lord. For the last ten minutes, I will meditate to listen to the Lord and hear what He wants to speak into my life.

This is an easy exercise to put into practice, and a great way to start building your spiritual discipline and endurance. Let's conclude with a prayer and honor the spiritual practice of communing with our Lord.

Dear Lord,
Thank You for the gift of your Word. Teach me to meditate on it day and night—not just reading it, but letting it sink deep into my heart. Help me to reflect on Your truth, to speak it over my life, and to live according to it. Let your Word shape my thoughts, guide my actions, and draw me closer to you. As I quietly ponder your promises and commands, may I grow in wisdom, strength, and obedience. Help me delight in your Word and treasure it more each day.
Amen.

CHAPTER 10

ANTICIPATE PAIN WITH PURPOSE

Pain is a humbling experience—because it exposes our shortcomings, limitations, and weaknesses. Breaking one of your bones doesn't happen every day (thank goodness), but when it does, you're quickly reminded just how breakable, in a sense, that you are. Break even a toe and you won't be walking as nimble nor moving as quick as you usually are. (And trust me, I've broken both my pinky toes!) And if you break a leg? At the bare minimum, you'll be in a cast with crutches. Whether you want to ask for help or not, you're immediately put in a position to need it, which is also humbling. Shopping at the grocery store, cleaning your house, and walking around in general suddenly become a lot easier if you have some help.

The same holds true with our mental health as we navigate the most painful moments during the healing process. There is suffering that comes with a mental illness, and if we choose to heal, we will not experience immediate relief from our pain. As we've established, we must go through pain to get to the other side of it in the healing process. But when we understand the purpose, the pain becomes *purposeful*. We can see the end goal—to become whole—and we know how to get there.

In our wholeness, we can fully love God and love others. In knowing that, our pain takes on a different form—one with exponential benefits.

In a World of Trouble

Scripture doesn't tell us we won't suffer; quite the contrary—it tells us to *expect* it. Misinterpretations of the biblical concept of blessings, cherry picking verses from the Bible, and prosperity Gospel teaching have all unfortunately helped promulgate the idea that Christians won't suffer. But that's just not a biblical teaching. Jesus Himself tells us in the Gospel of John that "in this world you will have trouble" (16:33). The Bible consistently teaches us that, as believers, we will experience hardship, trials, and suffering, often precisely *because* of our faith.

But there is more to that verse in John, and we aren't left without hope. The full verse in John 16 reads, "I have told you these things, so that in me you may have peace. In this world you will have trouble. But take heart! I have overcome the world" (v. 33). Jesus leaves us with *eternal* hope. In these verses, Jesus is concluding what's become known as His Farewell Discourse, His final teachings before His arrest. He begins, "I have told you these things" (16:33). The "things" he's reminding His disciples of is all that he's been teaching them, preparing them for His death and resurrection.

Jesus continues, telling them He is going away, but not abandoning them. He promises to send the Advocate (Holy Spirit) to guide, teach, and comfort them (John 14:16-17, 16:7-15). Then, He tells them they will face opposition and suffering. He's been nothing but honest about that, of course (John 16:2, 20), but He also promises their sorrow will turn to joy (John 16:22). He begins with *peace* and ends with *hope*. This is a powerful declaration about His victory over the fallen world in which we live, and He offers us hope beyond our suffering. Through His life, death, and resurrection, he's defeated any power of this world.

By entering into this world, Jesus entered into our suffering. But He came to offer hope for the here and now and hope for beyond this world. Jesus Himself is described as a man who "was despised and rejected by mankind, a man of suffering, and familiar with pain" (Isaiah 53:3). As Christians, we participate in the same sufferings as Jesus did. And it is through those sufferings that God works to form Christlike character in us.

A Purpose in Pain

It would be unfair—and untrue—to attribute all pain to having one purpose. The overarching reason we experience suffering is because we live in a fallen world. It is caused by sin, hatred, persecution, death, evil—all parts of living in that fallen world. It is just part of living. But while we don't get the choice to affirmatively opt out of pain, we do get a choice in how we handle it. Understanding that begins with how we view what we can do with our pain.

James tells us, "Dear brothers and sisters, when troubles of any kind come your way, consider it an opportunity for great joy. For you know that when your faith is tested, your endurance has a chance to grow." (1:2-3, NLT). James isn't one to sugarcoat the truth. Notice, first, that James says "when," not "if" troubles come your way. But then, He tells us to see trouble as an opportunity. He isn't saying we should enjoy suffering. Instead, he's encouraging us to see it differently—not as pointless pain, but as a spiritual opportunity. Suffering itself isn't joyful, but the growth it produces is.

When held up next to this passage in James, we can see the pain that comes with healing as one of opportunity—not one to enjoy, but to view with purpose. Romans 3 tells us as much the same, saying that trouble has meaning: "we also glory in our sufferings, because we know that suffering produces perseverance; perseverance, character; and character, hope" (Romans 5:3-4). Pain and suffering can produce growth, developing us as stronger believers in our faith.

The Fruit of Pain

If you ever learned the Fruits of the Spirit by singing the song, you probably still hear it in your head when you read through the list: love, joy, peace, patience, kindness, goodness, faithfulness, gentleness, and self control (Galatians 5:22–23). Some of these biblical words have greater meanings, and I love how the other translations of the Bible outline their variants. Here are some that should be noted.

These nine qualities are the nine spiritual fruits (what the Holy Spirit's presence produces us):

- love / disinterested dedication for others
- joy / gladness
- peace (interior and exterior)
- patience (both in the capacity to wait and also to maintain the correct attitude while waiting
- kindness / gentleness
- faith / faithfulness
- meekness / humility
- self-control / temperance.

Seasons of hurt, sadness, and pain are planting seasons, opportunities to produce these fruits. In other words, pain can produce the fruits of the Spirit in us.

When we are in pain, all we have to do is ask for help. Hebrews

13:5 records God's promise that He will never leave us—never. So we are not alone in our pain. First, we must surrender—not ourselves to our pain but our pain to the Lord. Then, we must persevere through our pain, which is where the Holy Spirit comes in. The Holy Spirit comes alongside us to be our advocate, and as we walk in step with the Spirit, we deepen our dependence on God.

Our responsibility is to respond with faith and obedience, and the Holy Spirit empowers growth of spiritual fruit. We bear the fruit, and the Holy Spirit produces the growth. Our pain, troubles, sufferings, and struggles become the soil where the fruit of the Spirit can truly grow. When we suffer, we are given an opportunity for the Holy Spirit to shape us—producing patience as we wait, kindness in how we respond, and self-control when we're tempted to give up.

The twentieth chapter of Proverbs touches on some of those fruits with some searing imagery. Its thirtieth verse reads, "Blows and wounds scrub away evil, and beatings purge the inmost being." Ouch. Talk about pain. The verse obviously isn't endorsing abuse, but it is pointing out that pain can purify our character. Its brutal imagery shows that painful experiences can reach the deepest parts of who we are and bring about meaningful change. Pain presents us an opportunity that, if taken, can lead to inner growth and transformation. It's an opportunity that reveals and refines our character. And we often gain insight and maturity through pain we'd never learn in any other way.

The Benefits of Pain

When Paul wrote to the church of Galatia, He asked them a direct and to-the-point question that—if I were to guess—likely stopped them in their tracks. The Galatian church had digressed to trying to earn righteousness rather than living by faith in Christ. To get them back on track, Paul reminds them of their past suffering. He asks, "Have you experienced so much in vain—if it really was in vain?" (Galatians 3:4). Essentially, he's asking, "Have you gone through all of this for nothing?" Paul's question is one for us all: are we going to waste our suffering? He's implying that if we have to go through pain and suffering, we might as well put it to good use.

One way to use our pain beneficially is to come alongside others in theirs. You may serve as an encouraging mode to someone else simply by choosing to heal, and even more so as you persevere through it—perhaps without ever even knowing. Someone may be watching you from afar, someone you barely even know. But they know enough to how you're modeling healing, and it may be just enough for them to begin their own journey.

The first official run I ever did, I got paired with Jaime Garcia to run it. That's right—Major League Baseball champion, the Jaime Garcia. Wonders never cease. But truly, being partnered with Jaime, my friend and one of the best athletes I know, was another glimpse of God's grace. When we got connected, I'd been needing a pat on the back from someone who was ahead of me in the sport of running, someone who knew more than me, and someone who had already run the path I was just starting out to run.

Then God put a great athlete to run alongside me. Jaime could have easily completed three laps on any track while I was taking my first three steps. But Jaime kept pace with me. He set the tone for our run, but he allowed me to set the pace. Jaime allowed himself to be used by the Lord without even knowing it. I told Jaime this in an informal interview we did back around that time—thanked him for letting the Lord use him. I was shocked by his response because, in a turn of events, he thanked me.

"You don't know how much I appreciate your words, your

vulnerability. I know that all the people who follow you are extremely blessed, and I admire you so much. I think the blessing is mutual. This helps me and inspires me a lot to keep going," he said. I already knew Jaime to have such a soft heart, but his words really stopped me in my tracks—or, on the track, so to speak. There I was, totally out of my little league to have someone from the major league (literally) thank me.

This goes to show that you never know how God can use your pain, which is part of your story, to bear witness to the world. You don't have to get on a stage or shout about it. But just by living your life, speaking openly about your journey, healing, and Lord's work in your life, you can bear witness. All of it is a testimony that someone needs—someone who will be great for your testimony, heart, and vulnerability. The enemy enjoys using the pain of this world to distract us from Jesus. But we can redirect our negative emotion to the enemy. Jesus overcame the enemy, and when we choose to share our story—our testimony—we join in that overcoming. In that freedom, one way to continually overcome the enemy is by sharing our story, by testifying about our overcoming.

Sometime ago, I realized that I had been wasting my pain. The day after Christmas of 2021, just three weeks after successfully running my first Chrisitne D'Clario 5k Race, I had an accident and fractured my tailbone. At that point of my life, I had made strides with taking back my health. All the elements of my being—the heart, soul, mind, and strength—were finally coming into alignment. And in that alignment, I had achieved being fully pain-free after years of inflammatory responses to high stress and trauma triggers. And then, bam! I couldn't walk without being in excruciating pain with each step. It was a literal pain in the behind.

As my recovery advanced and I was able to carefully leave my house again, I went straight to church. There was a conference that night, and Pastor Rick Warren was the speaker. But he was speaking via a pre-recorded video, because, as it turned out, he was also facing some very painful health issues. When he began his opening remarks of the sermon, there I was, sitting on a donut cushion and feeling the consequential throbbing pain of my literal first steps outside of my home. Remarkably, his sermon was all about the benefits of our pain.

At hearing the title of the sermon, I felt a wrestle inside of me. On one hand, I wanted to roll my eyes and say, "Really? Benefits in pain? There are none!" On the other hand, I felt myself drawn to lean forward and absorb whatever wisdom I could from a sermon with such a provocative title. I chose the latter, and I'm so glad I did. That evening, so many paradigms shifted for me. Ever since, every time I have experienced pain or counsel someone who is in pain, I have employed many of the principles I learned that night. That sermon ignited sparks within me to deepen my understanding of the benefits of pain. And much of what I share in this chapter was birthed out of that deepened understanding.

Pain is a powerful witness to the world because it can connect others who are suffering to the love of Jesus. As Paul writes in Philippians 1:12, hardship can advance the gospel. Your deepest life message is often born out of your deepest pain. Instead of hiding your hurt, let it become a testimony someone else needs. When we patiently endure trials, we reflect the strength and grace of God. The greatest evidence of God's love wasn't comfort—it was Christ's suffering. So don't waste your pain; let it be a light that points others to hope and redemption.

Pain also draws us into deeper fellowship—with others and in serving them. When shared honestly, pain breaks down walls and creates connection. We are called to carry one another's burdens, and that "fellowship of suffering" (Galatians 6:2) is a sacred space of love and support. You will find that often, words aren't even needed; your presence alone shows your love. Pain matures compassion, enabling you to serve others more tenderly. God comforts us not just for our own healing, but so we can comfort others (2 Corinthians 1:4-6). Your hurts may become evidence of your redemption in the eyes of others.

There is no doubt too that pain can make us more compassionate and sensitive in serving others—what some call redemptive suffering. When we've experienced deep hurt, we're often better equipped to recognize and respond to the pain of others. God comforts us in our troubles so that we can comfort others with the same comfort we've received (2 Corinthians 1:4-6). Our suffering isn't a waste; it can become the very tool God uses to bring hope and healing to someone else. It is often through pain that we learn to serve with real compassion, just as Jesus did.

Taking Heart

We are called to live fully and abundantly. Scripture tells us that Jesus came not only to offer eternal life, but to give us a rich, meaningful life here and now: "The thief comes only to steal and kill and destroy; I have come that they may have life, and have it to the full" (John 10:10). This abundant life includes spiritual depth, healthy relationships, and purposeful living. While we look forward to the promise of heaven, that hope should not cause us to disengage from the present or use eternity as an escape from the challenges of this life.

Instead, Scripture teaches that even suffering holds purpose. Pain can become a space for growth, character formation, and spiritual maturity. Choosing to heal in the face of hardship isn't weakness—it's strength. It requires courage, resilience, and often faith that God is doing something meaningful even through our hardest moments. Abundant life doesn't mean a pain-free life, but a life lived deeply—with God, with others, and with hope.

Finding purpose in our pain gives us a perspective that helps us not only to survive, but to live abundantly—even in the midst of the most difficult times.

CHAPTER 11

MAKE SPACE FOR OTHERS

When I blurted out the unfiltered truth of going through the darkest season of my life on the radio interview, I had really just started my healing journey. I was meeting with my therapist regularly, and in our next session, she asked me how I felt after having spontaneously shared such an intimate part of my life. I answered, but tacked on a question that had been parading around in my mind.

"I feel relieved. But why? Why do I feel relief?" I hadn't been able to figure that out. I'd anticipated having lots of emotions after publicly unveiling what was really going on behind the closed doors of my life. Relief wasn't one of them.

"Confession," she said, "brings healing. The more people know what's hidden, the less power the enemy has to condemn you. And the more healing can flow into your life."

"Then let's confess it to the world," I replied. And I meant it.

So, that same week, I decided to make a confessional video and post it on YouTube. In it, I explained everything that had happened in the lead up to my diagnosis and everything I'd experienced since. Before posting it, I still had no idea what the response would be. Maybe people would be receptive. Then again, maybe not. I hoped the response would turn out similar to the one I'd received during the radio interview. I still wasn't sure, but if this could give the enemy less power over me, I was all about it. With hopes of more healing ahead, I posted it.

To my surprise, I received more DMs and comments than I knew how to handle. I got thousands of them. Thousands. As

I read through them, two prevalent themes became overwhelmingly obvious to me.

One theme involved encouragement for me. People commented to tell me that they had gone through the same thing, and they wanted to encourage me to press on. These messages were a balm to my spirit and soul. I had known I wasn't one of only a few people in the world who had dealt with mental health issues. My midwife and therapist had made that very clear to me. But these messages were a kind of personal evidence of that. And here were all these people affirming my decision to heal. I was encouraged and felt more motivated by them.

The second theme involved encouragement for others. This theme hit my heart—and hard. In my video, I'd said something to the effect of, "I need help, and if you need help, it's ok to ask." That idea had resonated with people because I received countless messages that read, "You encouraged me to seek help." I hadn't expected this. I'd gone into posting this video to take power away from the enemy in my own life and to open more space for healing in me. It had taken a little courage to go through with it, but I was realizing that the courage it took me to tell my story had diffused out to others. By sharing my story, I had encouraged others to get help and have courage to start healing.

Once I knew sharing about my healing journey would not only help me but help others too, I knew there would be no stopping me. With my strength relying on God and my eyes focused on Christ, I had a new mission before me: to help prepare the way for others.

Words of Encouragement

If you've ever heard of the five love languages, you've probably heard of words of affirmation as one. *The 5 Love Languages: The Secret to Love That Lasts*, published in 1992 by Dr. Gary Chapman, describes five primary ways people give and receive love.[51] The concepts in this book are taught all over the place—churches, colleges, small groups—to help people improve communication in relationships by understanding how they give and receive love. Words of affirmation, specifically, are verbal expressions of love, appreciation, encouragement, or support that make someone feel valued and emotionally connected.

When I decided to run a 5k, I didn't have an official date set for when I would do it. But I committed to it by telling the world I was going to run one. (And by world, I mean Instagram.) I'd hop on to give updates after I finished a run, and I remember feeling such gratitude for all the folks who were so supportive. They would send such words of encouragement in the comments, and I was astounded at the love and support I received. It became true motivation for me—true blessings to my heart.

Whether words of affirmation is your primary love language or not, words of encouragement affect everyone. They give us motivation to begin a task or continue with one. They spur us on and help us to persevere. Proverbs 16:24 says, "Gracious words are a honeycomb, sweet to the soul and healing to the bones." Words reach all the way to our soul and deep within us to our bones.

A short article appeared in *Guideposts* several years ago titled, "The Power of Words."[52] Its author tells a cute story about her

---

51. Chapman, Gary. *The 5 Love Languages: The Secret to Love That Lasts*. Revised and updated edition. Chicago: Northfield Publishing, 2024.

52. "The Power of Words." *Guideposts*. Accessed July 17, 2025. https://guideposts.org/positive-living/friends-and-family/parenting/children/the-power-of-words/.

daughters, who had been listening to the sermon during "big service." She realized this when her four-year-old said her sister was "making bad confessions" over her. In retelling this lighthearted story of her daughter having grasped the concept of "the power of words," she explains that we should "take every opportunity to use your words to encourage and uplift the people you encounter each day."

As she reminds readers, Proverbs 18:21 tells us that "the tongue has the power of life and death"—a considerable responsibility for such a tiny part of our body. But words carry significant weight with everyone. She concludes that "others' words can deeply affect us, but our words can also deeply affect others." And how true that is.

When discouragement would come around during my healing journey, as it sometimes did, I would often turn to the Psalms and read David's words of encouragement. David was often writing to God, but He also spoke to Himself—to encourage Himself. I have returned to the words he spoke to Himself to use as encouragement for myself countless times. I still do and forever will—because his story has encouraged my own.

Words carry immense power. A single phrase of encouragement can lift someone's spirit, restore their motivation, and give them confidence. In moments of doubt or difficulty, kind and affirming words often carry more weight than we realize—echoing long after they're spoken. Whether it's a quiet reassurance or a heartfelt compliment, encouragement has the ability to heal, inspire, and change the weather in someone's season, if only for a day. Words spoken with great care can be a powerful act of love, one which we can all give to others.

Stories as Encouragement

Before they entered the Promised Land, Moses reminded the Israelites of their journey, of how far they had come. This is the central theme of the book of Deuteronomy. In his farewell address, Moses recounts God's faithfulness, saying, "Remember how the Lord your God led you all the way in the wilderness these forty years" (8:2).

They had discovered their voice from within the desert. The Israelites had begun to express their identity, fear, praise, and concerns more openly—a formative stage in discovering their voice.[53] They had *cried out with their voice while inside* the desert. Repeatedly, they cried out—sometimes in exhaustion, sometimes in fear, other times in desperation or repentance.[54] They had *prepared the way using their voice through* the desert. Their speech—praise, testimony, confession—began to shape their identity and prepare the next generation for life in the Promised Land.[55]

The years the Israelites spent making their way through the desert became a season of spiritual preparation. As they were wandering, they were simultaneously preparing to enter the Promised Land as one nation, a whole people. This season became a major part of their history, and it is history we read to learn from today. Israel prepared the way for us by giving us a story from which to glean wisdom. They were preparing the way for others—you, me, and every believer to come.

In the same way, our desert periods can become stories that prepare the way for others. Whether you've just started your healing journey or you're considering embarking on one, that is

53. See Exodus 15:1 and 19:8 for Israel's first communal praise and response to God.

54. See Exodus 16:2-3, Numbers 14:1, and Numbers 21:7 for Israel's concerns, fears, and confessions.

55. See Deuteronomy. 6:6-7, 32:1-2, and 27:14 for the teaching and worship instruction given to Israel.

something worth thinking about now—because your story can impact others and prepare the way for them to heal after you.

What we say to others can even shape their choices, decisions, and trajectory. This is the case when we pass along an encouraging word or two, but it is also true when we share our stories—honestly and with intention. We invite others to learn from our journeys and see their own more clearly. Our words become bridges of empathy, courage, and connection. Our voices can bring light and strength to others who may be walking through a dark desert.

Running With Forks

When I'm in the middle of training for a run, I'll come up against a few days when I have to run consecutively every now and then. This isn't as big of a deal now compared to when I first started running. As your body adapts to running over time, it generally becomes more efficient; you burn fewer calories doing the same run as you did when you first started. But back in those early training days, my body hadn't adjusted to my workouts.

After one early training day, I was famished. We were out of eggs at home (my favorite source of protein after a run), so I jumped in the car to go buy some. But I didn't make it to the store because I was getting hungrier by the minute. So I pulled into a restaurant to get some food in me. Mind you, this restaurant serves salads. I was making an effort to eat healthy too!

I stood in line, ordered my salad, and grabbed my little take-home bag once they'd finished my order. I was so excited, I practically danced across the parking lot. I made it to my car—having long surpassed the "super hungry" phase—and much to my dismay, I realized I had no utensils. So, back into the restaurant

I went. I checked that little area where they keep napkins, utensils, and cup lids, but all I saw were spoons and knives. No forks. I headed over to the counter and poked my head around where I could get someone's attention.

"Do you have forks? I didn't see any in their usual place. Can I have a fork?" I asked politely, though I was practically trying to talk louder than my stomach was growling.

"Oh, we're low on forks. In fact, all our stores are low on forks," replied the worker. "You'll have to eat with a spoon."

A spoon? I thought to myself. How am I supposed to eat a salad with a spoon? That's not going to work!

Silly as it may have been, it seemed bizarre to me that a place known for selling salads didn't have forks. But the more I thought about it, the more I started to see this same exact scenario in other situations. The one that I kept coming back to was the Church.

When people come to a church, especially if they are in a desert season, they are looking for hope—for light in darkness. They are searching for someone who is a reflection of Christ, someone who will help them to find their way out of the desert. The guides that life has offered have been unhelpful, creating only more difficulty. So they try a different route, one they've heard is meant to help. They arrive within the four walls of the building amid a congregation of people, but they find that there are no guides there either. Instead, they're met by figurative pointing fingers. Too often, they are met with judgment and condemnation—far from an invitation to come closer to Christ.

When I put these two scenarios together, I felt convicted. Am I being a good utensil to help someone eat from the fountain of life? Someone who is desperately longing for Jesus? Am I representing the love of Jesus by guiding others to His presence? Or, am I letting life get in the way? Am I too caught up in my own circumstances and unable to see others in need? Am I missing opportunities to bring people to a table full of spiritual food? Are they not eating because I, the utensil, am not serving them by being present in their situation?

Just as you need a fork to eat a salad, the world needs the children of God, those who are filled with the Holy Spirit, to help others eat from a table that brings life. When your desert season comes to an end, remember why your journey out of it began: so you can love others with your whole being. Many of those "others" are still in the desert. They may be people close to you or people you haven't even met yet. Their desert may look vastly different than yours. But no matter who, where, or how they are, we are to embrace them in love.

We need to show God's love in everything and to all people. Healing, as we'll recall, is a continual process. You choose to heal so that your being will be whole; then, you continue healing—never forgetting your journey in the desert.

When it comes time for you to be the utensil, serve others from a table full of spiritual food—be the facilitator, be present.

PART IV

A VOICE TO LOVE GOD—OUT OF THE DESERT

TRANSFORMATION

CHAPTER 12

WITH ALL YOUR HEART

Our heart is the origin source of emotions and life—in a literal sense. God created our hearts as the center of our bodies. Functionally and symbolically, the heart's central location reflects its essential role in sustaining life. And emotions are at the center of an abundant life.

First, the heart's functional importance. Your heart is located in the center of your chest. (Well, technically, slightly to the left.) That's because it's the most efficient position for it to pump blood throughout your entire body. That allows it to get oxygen to your head, organs, legs, and arms while remaining protected behind your ribs. It plays a part in digestion, temperature regulation, and general body function, and your tissues and organs get nutrients thanks to its work.

Second, the heart's symbolical significance. The heart has long symbolized the emotional center of a person. We think of love, compassion, courage, grief, and other emotions as coming from our heart. That's because when we experience intense feelings, we often feel a physical sensation in our chests. We sense a racing heart when we're nervous, an aching heart when we're sad, and a steady heart when we're calm.

The Bible presents emotion as a natural and meaningful part of human life—rooted in our hearts. Emotions like joy, sorrow, fear, anger, and love are all acknowledged in Scripture, but the Bible teaches that they should be guided by faith and wisdom. The heart is the center of inner life: "Above all else, guard your heart, for everything you do flows from it" (Proverbs 4:23). This verse is not instructing us to avoid emotions and try not to feel them because they're dangerous. It *is* instructing us to be mindful about what influences our heart—because our thoughts and actions are influenced *by* our heart.

It's no wonder that your heart, the seat of your feelings and emotion, is first on the list in Scripture with which we are instructed to love God wholly.[56] Could it be a clue that the starting point to learning to love fully is to learn to regulate our emotions? Have you ever loved someone so deeply and, as much as you try to express it properly, dysregulated emotions get in the way of giving or even receiving love? I know I have. Certainly, an unruly heart is a major hindrance to fully expressing our love.

Our emotions themselves are not wrong. They're part of how God created us. But because they are powerful, Scripture calls us to steward them wisely, aligning our hearts with God's truth so that our emotions support, rather than derail, our spiritual and emotional well-being.

Emotions as Signposts

The heart has historically been considered the center of emotion and the mind the source of reason, especially since the Enlightenment (which peaked in the eighteenth century). This split started way back with Greek philosophers—think, Plato—who basically dubbed the mind superior to the heart. Generally speaking, these philosophers put more stock in reason and logic than feelings and heart.

In part, that's why our culture today tends to associate the heart with love, passion, vulnerability, and the like. It's also why

56. Deuteronomy 6:5; 10:12; 11:13; 30:6; Joshua 22:5; Matthew 22:37; Mark 12:30; Luke 10:27

emotions are sometimes cast in a bad light: when they're put up against logic, they're seen as less trustworthy. There is some truth to this. As I've mentioned many times over, we shouldn't base our actions solely on emotion, *but* we should honor them and understand what they're telling us.

It's helpful to think of emotions as guideposts rather than greenlights *or* road hazards. They give us information we can use to navigate life. Brené Brown explains emotions not as weaknesses to avoid but "signposts" that guide us toward courage and connection.[57] Courage isn't about finding strength to squash our feelings. It's about being vulnerable in expressing our feelings honestly. This kind of courage is foundational to healing. When we can identify and name what we're feeling, we can move through those emotions with greater clarity and purpose. We're better equipped for the healing journey and life with authentic relationships thereafter. We heal our heart for the purpose of loving others.

As I mentioned in the first chapter, my heart has never known how to feel lightly. As someone who feels deeply, I know from experience that my emotions can significantly influence my thoughts and actions. But I have learned that basing my thoughts or behavior solely off my emotions is not healthy nor helpful. That is all the more reason to be aware of what I feel. Once I have an understanding of what I am feeling, I can ask myself questions that will redirect my thoughts. What am I telling myself? Is what I'm thinking true? Those questions then help inform my actions, behavior, and choices.

57. Brown, Brené. *Daring Greatly: How the Courage to Be Vulnerable Transforms the Way We Live, Love, Parent, and Lead.* New York: Gotham Books, 2012.

Optimism of the Heart

Optimists are typically highly regarded because they're known to have positive perspectives. An optimist as defined by the Oxford English dictionary is "one who expects or observes the most favorable outcome in any situation; a person with a hopeful and positive outlook."[58] Sometimes people only think of the latter when it comes to optimists, or, even further, that they only have a positive outlook because they ignore reality or put on a façade. But denying hard truths or pretending pain isn't real is not characteristic of a true optimist.

An optimist is someone who seeks meaning and purpose, *even in* painful circumstances. This true version of an optimist aligns with the biblical perspective of emotions. To experience the most positive, lovely, and life-giving emotions, we must experience the uncomfortable ones as well.

Experiencing all emotions is key to the abundant life Jesus wants for His followers, which He Himself modeled for us. Jesus felt an array of emotions. He felt gladness ("my joy" John 15:11), sadness ("wept" John 11:35), and anger ("in anger" Mark 3:5). Jesus did not solely act based on His emotion, but He allowed His emotions to give Him information. His anger, for example, was informative, not reactive, as we see right before He names the Greatest Commandment.

When Jesus arrives in Jerusalem with His twelve disciples (in Mark 11), their first stop is the temple courts, where His triumphal entry into Jerusalem swiftly becomes a scene of rising tension. Jesus had visited the temple courts just six months earlier, but money changers had apparently set up shop and turned

58. "Optimist." *Oxford English Dictionary*. Accessed July 10, 2025. https://www.oed.com/view/Entry/132434.

the courts into a marketplace during that time.[59] The temple was meant to be a sacred place of worship, but it had been turned into a marketplace of greed.

It doesn't take Jesus long to assess the situation: "On reaching Jerusalem, Jesus entered the temple courts and began driving out those who were buying and selling there. He overturned the tables of the money changers and the benches of those selling doves" (v. 15). According to Mark, He got right to it, driving out the buyers and sellers and clearing out the merchandise as soon as He walked in.[60] Jesus is angry, but this isn't a scene of out-of-control rage. His anger is a signpost, not a problem: it clarifies what matters to Him and what must be corrected.

On the opposite end of the emotional totem pole, joy was also very much a part of Jesus' emotional life. In Luke 10, Jesus expresses joy after seventy-two of His disciples return from preaching and teaching. They come back amazed, and Jesus celebrates not just their response, but God's power. He is delighted that God is revealing Himself to the humble and childlike. Scripture tells us that "at that time" Jesus was "full of joy through the Holy Spirit" (v. 21). God's will was being done and His kingdom was growing—and Jesus felt joy because of it.

To live the abundant life Jesus came to give us, we must live as He did, feeling and being aware of our emotions—because they are an essential part to that life. It's worth checking that your perspective aligns with that of a true optimist: one who is grounded in hope, practices acceptance, and finds good. All the while, your heart must be rooted in truth so that it, too, remains in check. With a healthy heart, you can give and love abundantly from it.

59. The last record of Jesus visiting the temple courts prior to Mark 11 is in John 7–10, when He attends the Feast of the Tabernacles in the fall. His Triumphal Entry in Mark 11 happens during Passover week in the spring. The time between the two is roughly half a year.

60. Mark 11:15-17

Getting Practical

I mentioned earlier that when I decided to heal, I took a practical approach. In keeping with that approach, I wanted to provide some guidance on two practical questions. But before presenting those, I first want to acknowledge their purpose: simply to be able to quickly assess where you are in your love for God. These lists are only a reference—not a judgment. They are not intended for you to judge yourself and feel guilt, or cast judgment and cause guilt. We are all human and healing.

That said, here we go.

What does it look like when you *are not* loving God with all your heart?

- *Attending church to check a box*

Going to church is absolutely a worthwhile practice to gather with other believers for worship, encouragement, teaching, prayer, and mutual support. But going to church for the sake of checking a box to meet expectations or maintain appearances lacks the intentional love and devotion God desires. Going to church is an important part of walking with Christ, but it is not the most important part. The heart of following Christ is a personal relationship with Him—marked by faith, obedience, love, repentance, and trust.

- *Going to God solely in times of turmoil*

We should absolutely go to God when we struggle. But if we are only going to God when times get hard, we have an unhealthy motive in our heart. Seeking God solely in turbulent times reflects a relationship of transaction, not relation. We should not *only* seek

God's help when we're in need or when life feels manageable. Instead, we should pursue Him in every season, including those that bring joy, calmness, and rest.

- *Refusing to let go of your desires*

Refusing to let go of our desires—especially when they conflict with God's will—can be a sign that we're holding back part of our heart from Him. If we are not submitting our desires to Him, we are not fully loving Him. We are to trust that His plans are better than our own, even in difficult seasons. No desire is worth turning into an idol or placing above God.

- *Attempting to force what you want (to control life)*

Trusting God's timing and sovereignty must come before fear, impatience, and even pride. Believing our plan is better than God's, even on a subconscious level, causes us to attempt to force what we want and control our own lives. We must surrender our desires and release our grip on control by believing God is both good and capable, even when His ways don't align with our own.

- *Creating a facade or filtering your prayers*

When we present a version of ourselves that's a façade or we filter our prayers in a way we think God wants rather than presenting our true selves, we're holding back trust and vulnerability. God already knows our thoughts, fears, and failures (Psalm 139:1–4), so we can trust Him by coming to Him honestly and unfiltered, just as we are.

- *Sensing obligation to His commandments*

When we obey commandments out of obligation, our relationship with God reflects duty more than devotion. Obedience is important, but we must come to understand His commandments come from love for us. They are not intended to simply instigate responsibility. Love comes first, and obedience follows naturally thereafter.

What does it look like when you *are* loving God with all your heart?

- *Cultivating a close relationship (beyond attending church)*

Loving God with all your heart means pursuing a relationship with Him that goes far deeper than just attending church. It's about drawing near to Him in your everyday life—seeking His presence outside the walls of a building. This might look like reflecting on His Word during a walk, pausing to acknowledge Him during a busy day, or simply being aware of His nearness as you go about your routine. Love grows through time, attention, and intention. Church is a part of that journey, but loving God wholeheartedly means inviting Him into all of life.

- *Communicating with Him regularly*

Our prayers don't need to be said in perfectly crafted words. But the habit of bringing your thoughts, struggles, gratitude, and questions to Him creates an ongoing conversation with God. Like any deep relationship, connection with God is nurtured through both speaking and listening. It's in this rhythm of conversation that our love for Him grows and deepens.

- *Shifting your priorities and motivations*

When you love God with all your heart, you naturally begin to reshape your priorities and motivations. Decisions that were once based on your desires are transformed. They become opportunities to reflect God in your life. It's not about abandoning ambition or joy—it's about aligning those things with a higher purpose: living in a way that honors Him. A good question to ask yourself when assessing your motivations and priorities is, *Of all the desires in my life, which of them brings the most glory to God? Which of them places me closer to God?* These help you determine what should come first.

- *Trusting Him with patience in faithfulness*

Loving God with your whole heart means learning to trust Him—even when you don't understand. This can be immensely difficult. It's choosing to remain faithful when prayers go unanswered or when progress feels slow. Patience becomes an act of love and surrender: a declaration that His timing is better than your own. But this love shows that it's not a love that's dependent on outcomes. Instead, it's rooted in who God is. Always faithful, always true, always making all things work together for our good.

- *Being vulnerable with Him, including your emotions*

To love God fully means bringing your whole heart—not just the neat or polished parts. God invites you to be honest with Him about your sadness, anger, fear, doubt, and joy. Vulnerability in prayer and worship shows that you trust God with your inner world, not just your outward behavior. Remember that God is great. Greater than your big emotions. Greater than your pain or past. He is strong enough to carry whatever we cast upon Him. He can handle anything.

- *Desiring to keep His commandments*

When you love God with all your heart, obedience becomes a joyful response. In the same way that we seek to please someone we are in love with, we also aim to please God and follow His instruction when we love Him truly. It's not about perfection; it's about living in a way that honors God. His commandments go from being restrictions on living to becoming wisdom for life.

CHAPTER 13

WITH ALL YOUR SOUL

Different from our heart, our soul is not something we can see or pinpoint physically. It's the invisible, inner part of us that gives life and identity. It is not tangible and temporary; the soul is eternal and spiritual. It is where our relationship with God takes root and where we experience conviction, worship, longing, and love. While we may not be able to locate the soul with our own little human tools, its presence is evident in our conscience and our longing for meaning. The soul is not confined to one place in the body. It is interwoven into the very fabric of who we are, forming the core of our being.

The original Greek word for "soul" in Mark 12 is *psychēs*, which means "life," "breath," or "spirit." Loving the Lord with all the soul is to be seen as loving Him with our "spirit man." This echoes the language of Genesis 2: "And the Lord God formed man of the dust of the ground, and breathed into his nostrils the breath of life; and man became a living soul" (v. 7 KJV). When God created Adam, He gave him life through His own breath—infusing him with a soul, a spiritual essence. When we talk about loving the Lord with all our soul, we are referring to loving Him with our spirit, our inner life, our God-breathed core—our spirit man. It's where deep connection and worship begin.

Our soul is not only the spiritual core of who we are; it is also the eternal part of us. It is uniquely the part of our being that will accompany us to heaven, the part that survives beyond physical death. Jesus affirms this in Matthew 10, saying, "Do not be afraid of those who kill the body but cannot kill the soul.

Rather, be afraid of the One who can destroy both soul and body in hell" (v. 28). Jesus reminds us that the soul holds eternal value and significance. To love God with all our soul is to entrust Him with the deepest, most lasting part of ourselves, acknowledging that our truest life is found in him.

Loving God with all our soul is about experiencing the fullness of life here and now. Jesus said, "I have come that they may have life, and have it to the full" (John 10:10). This "abundant life" is found in and created by the depth of our connection to God. When we love Him with our whole soul, we open ourselves to the kind of life Jesus came to restore—a life marked by peace, purpose, joy, and spiritual vitality. It's in giving our whole selves to him, especially our soul, that we begin to walk in the richness of life as God intended.

Spiritual Electrolytes

When I finished running thirty-five consecutive minutes for the first time, I was overjoyed. That had been my goal for quite some time. The first day I'd tried to make it thirty-five minutes, I hadn't been able to. I was disappointed, and I mentioned it to one of my recording engineers in the studio later that day. He's a dear friend and accompanies me in all my sessions in Dallas—and he also happens to be a runner. He gave me an electrolyte packet to put in my water and told me to give it a try on my runs.

The day I hit my goal, I'd done just that. I took large gulps of that electrolyte infused water at miles one, two, and three. I'd needed a boost each time I hit a mile. It seemed to give me this little burst of just what I needed to push through the pain in my calves, maintain regular breathing, and help me keep going.

After I came down from the excitement of hitting that goal, I got to thinking about those gulps I'd taken along my run. I had been drinking a ton of water before every run, intentionally staying hydrated—but it hadn't been enough to reach such a long goal. How many other times is this the case in life? How often do we do this spiritually, never giving our soul the water it thirsts for?

Sometimes we think drinking just a little water will be enough. We go to church on the weekends. We read a chapter in the Bible. We say a twenty-second prayer. Then, we expect that our tee-tiny sip of spiritual water will be enough to last us through the whole week. But as the week progresses, we start to fade—specifically, our soul starts to grow weary.

God gives us callings for our lives, with each one fitting who He created us to be. They are like seeds in our souls that grow beautifully with time, personal missions given to us with love and grace. These God-given assignments are part of the abundant life that Jesus wants us to experience—life that will bring glory to God. God sets goals of longevity before us, entrusting us with them to see them through. But those goals can't be fulfilled with just a little water—going to church on the weekends, hearing a sermon, or worshipping one time a week. We need *more.*

Thanks to that little electrolyte packet, I saw a parallel lesson between my spiritual life and my physical life. I wanted to reach bigger goals, stretch further, go longer. As I kept discovering how to nourish my body better, I started to see how to nourish my spirit better too. If I wanted to reach greater goals on my physical runs, I had to consume electrolytes. If I wanted to reach greater goals on my spiritual walk, I had to consume spiritual electrolytes.

We need more than just a little water to quench the thirst in our soul. We need those spiritual electrolytes that meet our needs more deeply. We need to seek the Lord in intimacy, go into a secret place, read His Word, savor it, study it. We need to pray more, spending more focused time with the Lord. Praying, meditating, reading, studying, fasting. Those spiritual electrolytes give us great spiritual nutrients to reach our spiritual goals, doing it all for the glory of the Lord.

Stirring of the Spirit

The Old Testament often refers to the "soul" as the innermost part of a person—the core of who we are. In Psalm 103:1, David writes, "Praise the Lord, my soul; all my inmost being, praise His holy name," showing that he sees his soul as his inner self, the part of him that worships and connects deeply with God. Our soul—our spiritual self—is not passive; it is aware of and responsive to God, capable of reverence, longing, and praise. It's from this deep place within that we are stirred to seek, know, and glorify him.

The New Testament often speaks of the soul as the part of us that is deeply and eternally connected to God. In Acts 2, the Apostle Peter delivers a powerful sermon on the day of Pentecost. He explains that Jesus is the Messiah, and he calls people to repent and be baptized. The crowd is deeply moved by his message, and their response shows it: "So those who received his word were baptized, and there were added that day about three thousand souls" (v. 41 ESV). They were "added" to the body of believers and became part of the growing community of Christ-followers, sharing lives of faith, worship, and generosity.

The emphasis in this passage is a spiritual one. The word "souls" emphasizes the individuals who were spiritually awakened and joined to God. Their souls became part of something eternal—because the soul is where our relationship with God is founded, both now and forever.

Our soul is deeply and spiritually connected to God. But we must commune closely and regularly with Him to accomplish the tasks He sets before us. We need to seek the Lord in intimacy—in a secret place, in His Word, in prayer.

Getting Practical

As with the "all your heart" questions, I am providing the same practical questions here once again. But again, let's acknowledge that these lists are only a reference—not a judgment. They are not intended for you to judge yourself and feel guilt, or cast judgment and cause guilt. We are all human and healing.

What does it look like when you *are not* loving God with all your soul?

- *Seeking man's approval, worldly pleasure, societal success*

When we prioritize the approval of others or chase worldly pleasures and status, our souls begin to anchor themselves in what is fleeting rather than in God. When worldly approval takes God's place, the soul becomes restless and detached from its true purpose—intimacy with Him. When God becomes the source of our identity and direction, we strengthen our souls' connection to Him.

- *Defining your worth to a career, money, performance*

Being tied to how well you perform, how much you earn, or what title you hold, often begins on a slippery slope. You don't start out thinking you're only as valuable as your achievements, but that's what your soul begins to sense. When a career, money, or performance becomes a measuring device, your soul detaches from the truth that you are deeply known and loved by God. God sees worth in who you are, not what you can prove or produce.

- *Worshipping solely when glad*

God created this life to be one that moves through seasons, and our worship to Him should be constant throughout them. Limiting worship to moments of gladness denies our soul the opportunity to deeply transform—transformation that can only happen when we turn to God at all times. Our soul's devotion to Him shouldn't be conditional because loving God with all our soul means choosing to praise Him in every season—not because life is always good, but because He is always good.

- *Ignoring Godly guidance or wisdom*

When we ignore God's voice—through His Word, the Holy Spirit, or wise counsel—we're basically saying our soul trusts its own way more than his. This can lead to spiritual distance from God, whereas seeking, receiving, and responding to His guidance draws our soul closer to him.

- *Focusing only on your values*

While having strong personal values isn't wrong, elevating them above God's truth turns the soul inward and often leads to self-centeredness or even compromise. When we filter faith through personal opinion instead of Scripture, we may cling to what feels right over what is right. When we surrender, we don't always understand His ways. They are, after all, higher than ours. But in surrendering, we allow God's character to shape our values and engulf our soul in the process.

- *Living for temporary gains*

Temporary gains like possessions, recognition, or even comfort can cause us to lose sight of what is eternal. But when we love

God with all our soul, we invest in truth, love, and people—always seeking to bring glory to God. Jesus taught us not to store up treasures on earth, but in heaven (Matthew 6:19-21), reminding us that the condition of our soul is tied to what we treasure most.

What does it look like when you *are* loving God with all your soul?

- *Finding fulfillment in God (not man's approval or worldly pleasure)*

When we love God with all our soul, our deepest satisfaction does not come from the approval of others or the pleasures of the world. Instead, we experience fulfillment from being in relationship with him. Human applause fades away and worldly pleasures disappoint us, but our soul remains anchored in the truth that only God truly satisfies.

- *Rooting your worth in God's love*

When we recognize our worth is firmly rooted in God's unchanging love for us, we no longer feel compelled to search for identity or validation in success, status, or performance. We learn to see ourselves through His eyes—as chosen, known, and deeply loved—and it frees us from the exhausting need to prove ourselves. We can live from a place of quiet confidence, in the presence of God.

- *Choosing to worship in all seasons*

When we love God deeply, worship becomes a constant practice in our lives, something we choose in every season. Whether we are rejoicing or struggling, our souls continue to turn to God in praise, because our love isn't based on circumstances. We trust that He is good, faithful, and worthy of our whole praise, no matter what.

- *Accepting His will over your own*

A soul fully loving the Lord learns to say, "Not my will, but yours be done." We surrender our desires, dreams, and plans, and we trust that His ways are wiser and better, even—or especially—when they don't match up with our own. This kind of surrender reflects a soul that trusts God's heart and leans into a relationship with Him at all times.

- *Prioritizing honoring Him*

When God has our whole soul, honoring Him becomes our deepest motivation. Our decisions, words, and actions begin to reflect a desire to bring Him glory. Perhaps most of all, we start to care more about what pleases Him than what pleases the world. Our souls are shaped by a longing to represent His character and extend His grace.

- *Maintaining an eternal perspective*

Loving God with all our soul gives us a clearer view of what truly matters. Living each day with eternity in mind changes everything about this life. When we can see this, our souls recognize that we have what lasts forever. This eternal perspective transforms every aspect of our lives, and we live knowing that our souls ultimately belong to God.

CHAPTER 14

WITH ALL YOUR MIND

As the divide between the mind and the heart deepened over the centuries, the mind grew to be recognized as the source of logic, control, and reason. Our heart, the source of emotion, gives us information to pay attention to, and our mind can frame those emotions with truth and rationality. They work together in this way.

The reason humans have inner experiences is because we have minds. When you see the color yellow, taste a chocolate bar, or feel a sense of joy, you're engaging with a personal, inner experience. Our mind is the defining mark of consciousness, the awareness of our thoughts, feelings, and experiences—our inner sense of being alive. Consciousness gives us a sense of identity over time because we remember past experiences. For better or worse, we use those experiences to create stories that we tell ourselves about who we are. But some of the stories we tell ourselves are not grounded in truth.

Thinking, I'm not good enough, could be rooted in a memory of having been rejected in the past. Believing, If I don't succeed, I'm a failure, may come from having been raised in a perfectionist environment. The thought, I have to make everyone happy, may have crept in after being in a relationship that implied love is earned. The belief, I am as valuable as I am accomplished, could stem from growing up not having enough. The list goes on and on—different for every person.

Sometimes, we don't even realize we're thinking these thoughts or holding these beliefs about ourselves. But we go about our lives operating as if they're true. You may not be walking around in your day-to-day life telling yourself, "I have to make everyone happy or no one will love me." But you may be running yourself ragged every day, attempting to appease everyone by doing for them to the nth degree—because you fear they won't love you if you don't. Acts of service are a beautiful, gracious blessing, but there's a fine line between generosity and self-neglect.

Letting go of the parts of the past that hinder us from healing will absolutely stir our heart, undoubtedly bringing up some uncomfortable emotions we must feel so they can pass through our bodies. But letting go of our past involves our mind too—because that's where our memories are stored.

Think about the notion of "letting go" in a different context. Let's imagine for a moment that you are in need of relocating. If you don't have an exorbitant amount of extra cash lying around, you have to sell your house to move to another at your new location. You have to let go of the house in which you are currently living in order to move to the house in which you are wanting to live. Maybe your family has outgrown your current house, and you need the extra space of a bigger place. Perhaps you are looking to upgrade to a newer neighborhood that has larger yards. Or maybe you just want something different, newer in general. So theoretically, you want to move to the new house.

But maybe you're also clinging to some parts of the current one—and not even in a nostalgic sense. The kitchen sink leaks, but you've become used to having to jiggle the faucet to the left to fix it. The floors are old, but you know exactly where all the squeaky or cracked spots are. The bedroom door slams shut too fast, but you've never forgotten that after it caught and broke your thumb a couple years ago. However, just because you've become accustomed to your current living situation doesn't mean you have to stay there, nor does it mean you haven't outgrown it. Either way, you can't move to the new while you're holding onto the old.

Your mind works much the same way. If you're ruminating on the past or replaying memories you've stored up over the years, you can't make way for new memories, a new season, a new story. We have to make space in our minds to allow healing to take place, a season of newness enter in, and a beautiful journey to ensue before us.

Mental Illness in Scripture

Mental health is important. *Hard stop.*

When we talk about mental health, we're talking about the health of our mind.

The Word of God does not gloss over mental health conditions, disorders, or illnesses. Scripture presents stories involving mental health episodes *and* addresses head-on how God treated those episodes. Let's take a look at some biblical examples of some of the mental health topics we looked at earlier.

Depression—Jeremiah, The "Weeping Prophet"

> *"Why did I ever come out of the womb to see trouble and sorrow and to end my days in shame?" (Jeremiah 20:18)*

Long after Moses' time, Jeremiah was called by God to be a prophet and he spent much of his life delivering messages of warning to the Israelites, especially the leaders and priests. He loved his people dearly, but they refused to heed his warnings more often than not—and he felt great sorrow for the majority of his life because of it. He continued faithfully delivering God's messages, but he's often referred to as "the Weeping Prophet." The first nineteen chapters of Jeremiah record his calling, ministry, and warnings. By Jeremiah 20, he's been rejected, ridiculed, and isolated. In verse 18, he expresses his anguish, curses the day he was born, and questions the purpose of his life. Those are deep, despairing thoughts and feelings.

This was a man who heard from God regularly, yet God didn't respond directly in that moment. Instead, He allows Jeremiah space to express his honest emotion and his deepest thoughts. Then, He continues to walk with Him through those thoughts and feelings. And looking at the whole of Jeremiah's story, we can see how God consistently cared for him. Scripture shows us that even the most faithful of servants wrestled with depression—and it doesn't shy away from telling us about that.

Suicide—Elijah

> *"He came to a broom bush, sat down under it and prayed that he might die. 'I have had enough, Lord,' he said. 'Take my life.'" (1 Kings 19:3-5)*

In 1 Kings 18, the Prophet Elijah experienced a great victory. In a spiritual battle against four hundred and fifty false prophets, God answered Elijah's prayer to send fire from heaven as evidence that God is the one true God. When Queen Jezebel heard about this, she immediately promised to kill him—so Elijah took off. He ran into the wilderness, and his discouragement caught up to him. He thought he was the only faithful one left (v. 10), so he believed his efforts had been in vain. Maybe he even thought of himself as a failure. He was disappointed (hurt), scared of persecution (fear), and grieved by the queen's refusal to repent (sadness). So, Elijah, a prophet of the Lord, sat under a tree and prayed he would die.

As we covered earlier, God sends an angel to care for Elijah, to bring him back to life. Then, God himself tells Elijah that he is not alone, that seven thousand others have not bowed to the false god. He assures Elijah that he is not the only faithful one. God spoke gently to him, telling him he was not alone and giving him renewed purpose.

Anxiety—David

> *"My heart is in anguish within me; the terrors of death have fallen on me. Fear and trembling have beset me; horror has overwhelmed me."* (Psalm 55:4-5)

David was always one to express his thoughts and feelings openly, which is why I return so often to the Psalms. In Psalm 55, he is overcome with feelings of fear and anguish because he has been betrayed. We don't know exactly who the betrayer was, but we know enough to discern it was a close friend, an advisor, or possibly even his son Absalom. He records his feelings of inner turmoil and emphasizes his fear of death. David's fear of death was definitely not unwarranted—King Saul had tried to kill him, he'd been a warrior in battle, he was betrayed by those closest to him, and his own son led a full-blown rebellion against him.

God responds to David's anxiety by hearing his prayer and giving him strength to continue on. In verse 22, David expresses his confidence in God: "Cast your cares on the Lord and He will sustain you; He will never let the righteous be shaken." David, in turn, trusts that God will deliver him and uphold those who remain faithful.

Grief—Job

> *"Why did I not perish at birth, and die as I came from the womb?" (Job 3:11)*

At the beginning of the book of Job, Job loses his wealth, his children, and his health—all in quick succession. He initially responds with worship and restraint, but by chapter 3, his suffering overwhelms him. Job wishes he'd died at birth to have avoided the pain he is enduring. He is in the throes of grief, and he longs for relief.

In chapters 38-41, God speaks to Job out of a whirlwind, yet He doesn't provide answers to Job's questions about his suffering. Instead, He reminds Job of His wisdom and control. God shifts the focus to His own sovereignty and the vastness of His purposes. In the end, God affirms Job's honesty, restores his health and fortunes, and blesses him even more than before. God shows that while He may not give direct answers in this life, He will always remain wise, just, and in control.

Stress—Paul

> *"Besides everything else, I face daily the pressure of my concern for all the churches."* (*2 Corinthians 11:28)*

1 and 2 Corinthians are copies of the Apostle Paul's letters to the church in Corinth. In 2 Corinthians 11, he's defending his ministry against people who were challenging him. By this point, Paul has endured many hardships while in his ministry; he's been beaten, put in prison, gone without food, survived in a shipwreck, and subjected to a whole lot of dangerous situations. Beyond the

physical danger he's been in, he carries a spiritual burden for the believers. In verse 28, he expresses a serious concern: he's stressed by the spiritual responsibility he feels to those believers.

God does not swoop in and tell Paul, "Nevermind about the calling I gave you." And He doesn't always remove Paul's suffering. But God does provide what Paul needs to endure it. In the next chapter, God tells Paul, "My grace is sufficient for you, for my power is made perfect in weakness." God meets Paul in his struggles and empowers him through them. He gives Paul strength, wisdom, and the ability to persevere and shows He will carry His faithful servants through their suffering, trials, and struggles.

When these biblical figures cried out to God in their distress, He did not always respond immediately, but He met them in their suffering and offered them strength. That is precisely the case with God's only son, Jesus, as well.

The night before His crucifixion, Jesus goes to the Garden of Gethsemane to pray, knowing the suffering He is about to endure. He kneels to pray, and the Gospel of Luke records it in chapter 22. He asks the Lord to "take this cup," making His request, but He ultimately concludes "not my will, but yours be done" (v. 42), desiring God's will over His own. Jesus is deeply, deeply distressed in this moment. He continues praying, and Scripture records His mind's state in sheer honesty: "And being in anguish, He prayed more earnestly, and His sweat was like drops of blood falling to the ground" (v. 44).

The phenomenon of sweating blood has actually been recognized in the medical world as a rare disease called Hematidrosis or Hematohidrosis. It occurs when people are in deep anxiety, fear, or excessive stress, though not physically injured.[61] The body

61. Octavius GS, Meliani F, Heriyanto RS, Yanto TA. Systematic review of hematidrosis: Time for clinicians to recognize this entity. World J Dermatol 2023; 11(2): 7-29 [DOI: 10.5314/wjd.v11.i2.7]

reacts to the psychological element of dread and terror-driven anxiety by over-driving the fight or flight stress response. This puts tremendous pressure on the tiny blood vessels that operate the sweat glands, causing them to rupture and blood to spill into the pores and cause bloody sweat.

Jesus knew the true terror and pain that he would have to live through by going to the cross. Yes, it put his body under tremendous duress. Yet He still chose to carry on with the plan of salvation. This moment reveals both Jesus' true humanity—feeling fear, sorrow, and distress—and His willingness to endure suffering out of love for the world.

God responds, but like many of the other biblical figures, He does not answer Jesus' request by removing the cup given to him. Instead, He responds by giving Jesus strength to endure, not escape: "An angel from heaven appeared to him and strengthened him" (v. 43). God's presence is with Jesus in the midst of His anguish. This is a pattern throughout the Bible: God may not take away the trial or suffering, but He provides support and strength needed to face it faithfully.

Mental Support

Way back in 1667, John Milton published *Paradise Lost*, a retelling of the biblical story of Adam and Eve in the Garden of Eden. One of the poem's most famous lines appears shortly after satan is cast out of heaven and into hell when he says, "The mind is its own place, and in itself can make a Heaven of Hell, a Hell of Heaven."[62] Here, satan's lines are a reflection of the inner workings of his will, his belief that he can control his suffering—using his mind. Through his dramatized depiction of satan, Milton

62. Paradise Lost, Book I, line 254.

highlights the pride in satan's attempt to control and, conversely, the power of God's sovereignty.

None of us have that kind of power—power to escape suffering simply by thinking our way out of it. We can take steps to heal our mind, steps on the journey toward mental health and healing, but we must also continually go to God for support along that journey. This is especially the case when we're given more than we think we can bear—which, at some point, you've probably heard won't be the case. The saying, "God won't give you more than you can bear," isn't actually Scriptural. (It's often confused with Scripture's declaration that we'll never be tempted beyond what we can bear in 1 Corinthians 10:13.)

Paul writes in 2 Corinthians that he was "under great pressure, far beyond our ability to endure, so that we despaired of life itself" (1:8). Even the Apostle Paul reached a point of despairing of life, of bearing more than he could carry himself. But Paul realized the point: "This happened that we might not rely on ourselves but on God, who raises the dead." (v. 9). Paul realized this was teaching him to rely on God *and* rely on help from other believers (v. 11).

Like Paul, when we experience more than we can endure on our own, we can depend on God to be our ever-present help *and* turn to believers He has placed in our lives as a source of strength. God created community to strengthen and help us: "I will remain in the world no longer, but they are still in the world, and I am coming to you. Holy Father, protect them by the power of your name, the name you gave me, so that they may be one as we are one" (John 17:11).

When you have tried to heal your mind without yielding results, seek help. Go to God, go to your community. Lean on those He has blessed you with to offer you help.

Getting Practical

As with the "all your heart" and "all your soul" questions, I am providing the same practical questions here too. But again, let's acknowledge that these lists are only a reference—not a judgment. These are not intended for you to judge yourself and feel guilt, or cast judgment and cause guilt. We are all human and healing.

What does it look like when you are *not* loving God with all your mind?

- *Dwelling on cultural influences*

When our thoughts are shaped more by culture than by Christ, our values and decisions begin to reflect popular opinion rather than biblical truth. You may become more concerned with trends, image, or success than with holiness, humility, or service. If we allow cultural voices to creep in, we start to define our identity, worth, and worldview by those voices instead of God's. This drift can be subtle, but over time, it leads to a mind that prioritizes what's temporary over what's eternal.

- *Agonizing over others' approval*

Shaping ourselves to fit other people's expectations comes from focusing on their approval. When our focus shifts away from what pleases God to what pleases people, we become consumed with others' opinions—for example, living for how many likes or views you can get on social media platforms, instead of living for God's will for your life. It's essentially undermining the freedom that comes from Jesus' love for us. This makes fully loving God with a clear, undivided mind nearly impossible.

- *Obsessing over control*

When we obsess over control, we reveal a lack of trust in God's sovereignty. Overplanning to manage outcomes and worrying all the while overwhelms our thoughts—when really, only God has control. You live in mental tension, trying to hold every piece of life together instead of resting in God's timing and wisdom, acknowledging Him as the Lord of your life. Many times, obsessing over being in control of everything goes hand in hand with the lack of rest and trust in God that we discussed in chapter seven.

- *Fixating on worries and fears*

Some worry or fear is a natural part of life, but when they dominate your thoughts, your mind becomes a battleground. Instead of anchoring your thoughts in God's promises, you rehearse your fears, which only allows them to grow—and, in turn, paralyze your faith. Fixating on fear distances you from the peace God offers and makes it hard to hear His voice through the noise. This is a matter of trusting God's goodness, provision, and control.

- *Ruminating on grudges and insults*

Holding onto grudges and rehearsing past insults traps your mind in cycles of bitterness and unforgiveness. Focusing on hurts hinders us from allowing us to freely meditate on God's grace. This mental state can poison your relationships and block your ability to reflect God's mercy and love. Ruminating on offense not only keeps wounds fresh but also distracts from growing in compassion, humility, and peace.

- *Neglecting biblical understanding*

If we aren't going to God's Word and being reminded of His truth, our minds can become easily swayed. We struggle to discern truth from falsehood. Without the steady influence of Scripture, your thoughts are shaped by emotion, opinion, or incomplete ideas of who God is. You're left vulnerable, confused, and unable to make wise choices. Actively seeking to know Him through His Word renews our thinking and helps shape our lives.

What does it look like when you *are* loving God with all your mind?

- *Reflecting on God's character*

Loving God with all your mind means regularly turning your thoughts toward who He is. He is a God of mercy, justice, power, and love. When you reflect on His character, you take time to recall how He has shown His character in Scripture and in your life. That allows you to shape your perspective and responses in a godly way, one that honors the Lord. This kind of mental focus gives you a sense of stability which leads to a natural outpouring of worship. You can trust when times are uncertain, because your mind is anchored in the unchanging nature of God. Developing the ability to anchor your thoughts on who God is regardless of your circumstance is a skill that makes us akin to having "the mind of Christ" as Scripture says in 1 Corinthians 2:15-16 and Romans 5:5-6.

- *Maintaining a goodness mindset.*

What you constantly think, you become. The more you think about good, Godly blessings, the more you become good, godly, and blessed. When you invite Scripture's trust into your daily thoughts and allow it to sink into your mind, you begin to reflect a deep love for the Lord. You stay mindful of God's promises and wisdom in your day-to-day life and allow Scripture to inform your approach to your days. It helps you view every situation through the lens of God's truth. The perfect rule of thumb on what you should be thinking of is in Philippians 4:8, "And now, dear brothers and sisters, one final thing. Fix your thoughts on what is true, and honorable, and right, and pure, and lovely, and admirable. Think about things that are excellent and worthy of praise."

- *Asking God for wisdom*

A mind that loves God seeks His guidance regularly, not just in crisis but as a way of life. You humbly acknowledge your limitations and turn to God in prayer, asking for clarity, discernment, and direction. You trust His wisdom is better than yours, and you ask for His wisdom as you make decisions. You lean into the confidence that His wisdom facilitates, each and every day.

- *Practicing faithfulness and trust*

Loving God with all your mind involves training your thoughts to rest in His promises even when circumstances don't align with what you had hoped. You can feel doubt and fear alongside your faith, trusting in God's control of your life and future. Your mental habits involve remembering God's promises, and your spiritual discipline involves remaining aligned with God's truth. You practice loyalty in both thought and action—even when it's hard.

- *Focusing on honoring God*

You are almost always thinking, *Will this glorify the Lord?* That question serves as a filter for your thoughts, which inform your actions. You consider how your choices, words, and priorities show God's presence in your life. This intentional focus leads you to think with purpose and humility, and you aren't swayed by the temptation to please people instead of God. He is your number one concern, the central aim of your thinking—not just on Sundays, but in the details of everyday life.

- *Studying and meditating on God's Word*

Loving God with all your mind includes a hunger to know Him more deeply through Scripture. You approach the Bible not just for knowledge, but to understand God in full and align your life with His will. You set aside time to study, reflect, and apply His Word, allowing it to transform how you think and live. Furthermore, beyond just reading and studying, it is the practice of meditation that ingrains the Word in our minds. Biblical meditation is to deeply contemplate, reflect upon, and internalize the truths and themes of Scripture. It is a focused and intentional way of engaging with God's Word, allowing it to soak into the heart and mind. It is not an emptying of the mind, as with other types of meditation practices, but it's a filling of the mind—with God's truth.[63] Meditation becomes a spiritual discipline that shapes your mindset and outlook. This pursuit of truth shapes your convictions, strengthens your faith, and deepens your love for God as He reveals himself through His Word.

63. Bible Hub, Meditation. Found at https://biblehub.com/topical/m/meditation.htm#:~:text=Definition%20and%20Context,the%20mind%20with%20God's%20truth.

CHAPTER 15

WITH ALL YOUR STRENGTH

Before I started training for a 5k, I'd started to feel like I was heading back to a period of emotional decline—as though I was about to do an about-face in the desert. I was experiencing high levels of anxiety and feeling this pervasive sense of sadness settle into my heart again. My body was asking—yearning, really—for an outlet to let go of all the stress I was holding in. I'd been harboring and holding onto all my pain, instead of paying attention to it and healing it. Running, I found, was a way for me to physically release stress by wrestling with my inner turmoil—and aim to win.

Meditating and praying while running gave all aspects of my life a totally different feeling. For me, if I had just been exercising to get in shape, I don't know that I would have ever grasped its spiritual benefit. That would have been lost on me. But I found that if I took that time to connect with God while exercising, I could submit my flesh and do it in the name of Jesus. It's similar to fasting because I'm submitting my flesh. When I run, I can meditate on His Word and on all the promises He has spoken over me that haven't been fulfilled yet, while, at the same time, I am physically moving forward. I can visualize the future, one step at a time.

I realized the parallel to my spiritual life—including its healing—is much like that of a physical race. At first, everything was exciting. I was getting into a new sport, putting on my running clothes and lacing up my tennis shoes, and I was also moving into a new journey of healing, readying myself for a season of newness. Then it got challenging. I faced hills, struggled with muscle cramps, and stretched my endurance. Simultaneously, I faced pain, struggled with courage, and stretched my ability to press on. At times, I didn't want to continue.

But with progress, there is always great reason to celebrate any victory with both healing and running. When you cross the finish line—of a race or a desert—you can celebrate. What an achievement those are—and what blessings flow from both! That has been immeasurably true in my life.

Move Your Body

Our body is the vehicle that our hearts, souls, and minds travel around in—the key word being travel. We are created for movement. Otherwise, God could have made us plants. We are created to *move* into action. Ephesians 2:10 says, "For we are God's handiwork, created in Christ Jesus to do good works, which God prepared in advance for us to do."

Stagnancy—whether physical inactivity or prolonged sedentary behavior—can gradually break down our body. In no particular order, here's what happens when we go without regular movement. First, our muscles weaken and atrophy, joints stiffen, and tissues lose their elasticity. That makes mobility more difficult but also causes us to be more susceptible to injury. Second, our circulatory system slows down. Oxygen and nutrients can't get to our cells as efficiently, which causes toxins to build up. Those toxins can cause us serious inflammation and physical pain. Next, our heart and lungs become less efficient, so we lose stamina in doing even daily activities, and our cardiovascular health plummets. Then, our brain is even affected. When we don't move, our blood flow decreases, and with it, the neurochemical activity in our brains does as well.[64]

64. de Lima, E. P., Tanaka, M., Lamas, C. B., et al. (2024). Vascular Impairment, Muscle Atrophy, and Cognitive Decline: Critical Age-Related Conditions. Biomedicines, 12(9), 2096. Found online at https://www.mdpi.com/2955430

When our body isn't active, our brain doesn't get what it needs to function at its best. You've likely already foreseen the writing on the wall here: this leads to lower mood and—you guessed it—increased risk of anxiety and depression. So, exercise is not just beneficial to our physical being; it positively impacts the mind as well.

Running has a plethora of benefits beyond just our physical health—and medical research and doctors have proven this to be true. So it's not a coincidence that the topic of depression and anxiety comes up in multitudes of conversations I have with people when we talk about running.

One day during the time of thriving in my newfound joy for running, I shared with my friend Christy Muller—a fellow author who is a licensed pastoral counselor with a specialization in neuroscience—that I had been feeling like my mind had been changing since I started running. (Not in the sense that I was changing my mind about what color top I wanted to wear that day, but in the sense that something was changing about my mind.) I told her that I was able to shift into a positive mindset with much more ease, regulate my emotions more consistently, and maintain a more focused attention span. I confessed to even desiring to eat healthier foods.

She shared something in return that blew my mind: regular physical activity, specifically running, increases neuroplasticity (the formation of new connections in the brain) and promotes neurogenesis (birthing new brain cells). And it happens *as* we are running. That meant I was quite literally rewiring my brain with each stride! Adding meditation on the Lord and His Word to the mix of that wondrous activity in my brain was truly transforming me.

I'd set out to kick my depression and anxiety in the face, figuratively speaking. As it turns out, I was working on literally kicking them both out of my brain.

Love Your Body

Loving your body doesn't just mean being happy with your physical appearance. It means respecting and caring for it, without harsh criticism or judgment. It means recognizing your body's value and appreciating what it can do—moving, breathing, feeling, healing. Loving your body entails treating it kindly with nourishing food, plenty of rest, and physical movement. It's about being grateful for the body you travel around in.

When I started running consistently, I wasn't training to lose weight—but that was a secondary benefit. I lost twenty pounds early on, but not because I was chasing a number. I didn't want to be "Skinny Christine." (Frankly, I was quite happy being Chunky Christine.) I wanted to be "Christine at her healthiest."

I've never really understood why the shape of our bodies matters so much anyway. Who decided what "healthy" looks like? Body fat percentage has nothing to do with how healthy a person is, and weight really doesn't have anything to do with health. Yes, there are conditions that can worsen with poor diet choices, like eating too much cholesterol or fat (though that's a different issue). But I know plenty of skinny people who are suffering on the inside—mostly because of medical conditions or high levels of stress.

In more recent years, as I have sensed my body getting older, my weight has fluctuated from time to time. You may identify the culprit as hormones, touring stress, juggling being a mom, wife, and head of many endeavors at once, or a number of other things called life. But no matter the number is on the scale, it is my responsibility to do my best to love my body, understanding that no matter how big or small I look, I am still a beloved child of the Most High God.

The only body you're responsible for is the one you see in the mirror. Pointing fingers at someone because of how their body looks—or because their body looks different from yours—is *not biblical.* A message of truth in love: we should not judge or condemn people for how their bodies look. You may not know the journey that has shaped someone's body, which may simply look different from the unrealistic standards often portrayed in the media. They could have thyroid problems, food allergies, hormone imbalances, or a different medical concern that affects their weight—none of which is a public matter, nor should it be. No one—absolutely *no one*—is in a position to judge or gossip about someone's outward appearance.

The beauty industry and the bikini market destroy people. They create psychological damage that hurts more than it helps. Sadly, this has made it nearly impossible for people to love their bodies—much because we've lost the true meaning of "love your body." Complicated by social media, perfection has become today's highest value—leaving insecurity in its wake and wreaking havoc on nearly everyone in one way or another.

One of the consequences has been a serious uptick in body dysmorphia, which is when someone becomes preoccupied "with an imagined or slight physical defect of one's body to the point of causing significant stress or behavioral impairment in several areas."[65] They may think their nose is too small, their skin too flawed, their physique too large, or their hair too thin. To them, it's a major flaw in appearance, but no one else sees it that way. At its core, body dysmorphia is a distorted perspective of self.

This may seem like a small matter, but it can cause major heartache in someone's life. It may start by avoiding social events, but it can lead to anxiety and depression—as can body shaming,

65. "Body dysmorphia." *Merriam-Webster.com Thesaurus*, Merriam-Webster, https://www.merriam-webster.com/medical/body-dysmorphia. Accessed 15 July 2025.

another major blocker to loving your body. Body shaming is "the act or practice of subjecting someone to criticism or mockery for supposed bodily faults or imperfections."[66] Telling someone, "You'd be so much prettier if you lost weight," body shames them, but it also implies their worth is tied to their body size. This is detrimental to anyone's mental health.

I like to imagine how Jesus would speak to people who take it upon themselves to freely critique the bodily appearance of others. If we were to paraphrase the "don't judge" Scripture in Matthew 7:1-5 and apply it to body shaming, it would probably read something like this:

> "Don't judge others, and God will not judge you. If you judge others, you will be judged the same way you judge them. *God will treat you the same way you treat others.* Why do you notice *the extra pounds, different body shape, distinct skin complexion, or unique imperfections* that your friend has, but you don't notice the *many imperfections about your own body, heart, mind, or soul*? Why do you say to your friend, 'Let me *tell you what you need to change*'? Look at yourself first! You still have *all those imperfect things to fix in your own self.* You are a hypocrite! First, take the wood out of your own eye. Then you will see clearly to get the dust out of your friend's eye."

This Scripture takes on a whole new meaning when we apply it to the language of our modern ways of judging, doesn't it?

Loving your body by caring for and appreciating it is an example of how the health of one part of the self can influence

66. "Body dysmorphia." *Merriam-Webster.com Thesaurus*, Merriam-Webster, https://www.merriam-webster.com/dictionary/body-shaming. Accessed 15 July 2025.

another. If we're meditating on truths in Scripture, then dwelling on cultural influences becomes less enticing, as does others' approval. This doesn't minimize the negative impact cultural influence can have on our self-image. And not caring at all about others' approval won't happen overnight. However, meditating on Scripture assuredly aids us in reframing how we think—including what we think of ourselves.

Scripture teaches that the body is valuable, created by God, and worthy of respect and care. 1 Corinthians 6 reminds us to care for our physical self: "Your body is a temple of the Holy Spirit… therefore honor God with your bodies" (vv. 19-20). Ephesians 5 reiterates the same message, encouraging us to care for our bodies: "After all, no one ever hated their own body, but they feed and care for their body, just as Christ does the church" (v. 29). Loving your body is an act of honoring God through how you care for it.

Psalm 139 gives us perhaps the clearest picture of the critical attention and intricate detail God gives to creating our unique, individual physical beings. David writes, "For you created my inmost being; you knit me together in my mother's womb. I praise you because I am fearfully and wonderfully made; your works are wonderful, I know that full well. My frame was not hidden from you when I was made in the secret place, when I was woven together in the depths of the earth. Your eyes saw my unformed body; all the days ordained for me were written in your book before one of them came to be" (vv. 13-16). Intentionally and intricately, God created each person. Our bodies and lives are reflections of divine craftsmanship. The concept of loving our body is rooted in the truth that we are wonderfully made by a loving Creator.

Fuel Your Body

A few years ago, in the midst of my inner healing journey, I found out I was allergic to gluten and corn—another thing I didn't know about for a long time. I'd simply had no idea.

When I discovered my gluten allergy, I also discovered a severe corn allergy along with it. I had adverse reactions to gluten—bloating, digestive issues, and a condition Dermatitis Herpetiformis, which is exclusive to people genetically incompatible with gluten. It presents as painful, itchy, micro-burn-like boils that take over a month to heal. And it became much, much worse for me when I ate anything with corn. (I'll spare you the intestine details.)

Recently, however, there's been an update to my gluten allergy. It started during lunch at the Franklin Graham and the Billy Graham Evangelistic Association's first crusade in Italy. I sat down next to the lady who had been serving as an Italian translator in the dining area with my little box of gluten- and corn-free pasta. (I know—in Italy!) She asked about my pasta, I shared about my gluten allergy, and the next thing I knew, we were discussing how God moves on Earth. We could sense His presence in the midst of our conversation, right there at our little corner of the table. When she asked if she could pray for me, I postured to pray without hesitation.

As she began to pray, we held hands and felt the embrace of God's presence over us. And her prayer brought me to tears. She gave thanks to the Lord and praised him for the blessing she believed me to be to the nations in God's name. She prayed for my family and work for the Lord. Then, as she was nearing the end of her prayer, she said these words that felt like a warm blanket over my soul: "Lord, would you please heal her of this gluten allergy so that she too can see *your* goodness every day, even by freely enjoying the food she is served when she is out ministering to you in her travel? We ask you please, in Jesus' name. Amen."

Most certainly, that mere sentence brought healing to me. But first, it healed my mindset in a way that I was unaware I needed it. Before that moment, I had accepted and resigned myself to knowing I would always have this allergy, the proverbial thorn in my side. But I had forgotten that, as God's child, I am allowed to come to His throne and ask for healing. My friend in Italy helped me remember that. I ate my first-ever Neapolitan pizza in the city it was invented that night. And I haven't experienced a symptom since.[67]

In one way, sharing this is tricky because I know you may be praying for healing from a particular ailment or allergy that you have yet to experience. But I'm not boasting about myself; I'm praising the great God I serve (1 Corinthians 1:31; 2 Corinthians 10:17). After all, you've read my story. You know my hardships. My life hasn't been a series of easy walks in every park every day. But God has always been beside me, in every park, on every walk, on every day. I'll share about the times God has given me strength in times he hasn't bestowed immediate healing, and I'll share about the times God has chosen graciously to heal me. In the good and in the bad, I give all glory to Him, whose ways are higher than mine. I will always declare the goodness of God—because *He* is good.

I am still holding onto hope that someday I will be healed from the corn allergy, God-willing. I know He can do it, and I pray He will.

67. Years of following a gluten-free diet taught me the benefits of avoiding inflammatory foods, so I still follow an almost gluten-free diet and try to keep it out of my diet.

It's no secret that balanced nutrition plays a vital role in both physical and mental well-being. There is even a direct connection between a healthy intestinal microbiota (the good bacteria in the digestive tract) and a healthy brain. Remember the HPA axis from Chapter Three? I mentioned that it helps manage your mood, immune system, energy levels, and even digestion. Physical activity adds a third benefit because it positively affects your microbiota and, in turn, positively impacts your brain.[68]

It's entirely possible to trade the negative physical and mental effects that come from poor nutrition for positive ones. Meal planning, for one, has helped me make more intentional, nourishing choices. It takes a bit more work on the frontend, but it pays off during the week—timewise and benefit-wise. When I meal plan, I don't usually find myself running through a fast-food chain because I'm caught in a bind. (They don't have forks sometimes anyway!) And I must give a disclaimer that this is something that I am still learning. It can get quite out of whack during heavy travel touring seasons.

Some foods are known to benefit brain health: berries, leafy greens, fish, and nuts. If you start regularly incorporating those types of foods into your diet, you can actually see an incline in your ability to focus throughout the day. If you want to be really intentional, you can keep a food diary to plan out your meals and keep track of what you eat. Again, this isn't for weight purposes. If you write down, for example, that Tuesday night at 6:00pm you ate pasta, and two hours later you notice your stomach is hurting, that's something to note. If that discomfort becomes a pattern, you might do some further research on sensitivities, such as how gluten may be affecting *your* body. If you look back in your food

68. Kang, P. & Wang, A.Z. (2024). Microbiota–gut–brain axis: the mediator of exercise and brain health. National Library of Medicine. Found online at https://pmc.ncbi.nlm.nih.gov/articles/PMC11096970/

diary and see that every time you have heartburn you've eaten pizza or marinara sauce, then you'll know tomato-based foods may not be the best choice.

Supplements are also something to consider, as the nutritional quality of our foods today has declined significantly in the last sixty years.[69] I recommend talking about this with your healthcare professional and getting on a supplement routine. I supplement daily and have noticed a positive change in my overall health since my body has the nutrients it needs. I use Vital Health supplement adaptogens and cannot sing their praises enough![70] Everything I take is to keep my body's systems well supported—including high-absorption multi-vitamins with probiotics (good gut bacteria), prebiotics (food for those good gut-bacteria buddies), aminoacids, superfood supplements, natural nootropics (to help brain function), and the best collagen (to help my skin stay healthy, especially in the sun). (Fun fact: Coconut oil works as sun protection for me too. When I used store-bought sunscreens, I always burned, turning red like a shrimp for three or four days, then I peeled. Coconut oil lets me get a nice tan and keeps my skin from being damaged by sun exposure. Add in some mineral sunscreen such as zinc oxide, and you've got yourself some great ingredients for natural non-toxic sunscreen!)

The more you nourish your body from the inside out, the healthier, and stronger you become! And let me tell you—the more you eat nutritious food, the more you will crave it. Fried, sugary, and generally unhealthy foods really do become less appealing. This doesn't happen instantaneously, but with time, change comes.

69. Bhardwaj, R.L., Parashar, A., Parewa, H.P., Vyas, L. (2024). An Alarming Decline in the Nutritional Quality of Foods: The Biggest Challenge for Future Generations' Health. National Library of Medicine. Found online at https://pmc.ncbi.nlm.nih.gov/articles/PMC10969708/https://pmc.ncbi.nlm.nih.gov/articles/PMC10969708/

70. Because Vital Health's supplements include so much that I love, I partner with them regularly and gratefully acknowledge their support.

Ultimately, this is a challenge of learning to listen to your body, especially at the start. Recognizing hunger cues, sensitivities, and how different foods affect your mood and energy are all key parts to developing a mindful approach to physical health and wellness.

Motivate Your Body

You can motivate your body by fueling it with proper nutrition, giving it consistent rest, and moving your body in a way that you enjoy. For me, that was running. But running isn't for everyone. If it's not for you, find an activity you love. Just make sure you are breaking a sweat doing something you like at least for twenty minutes, three times a week.

Some people love a group fitness class: dancing, pilates, barre, spin. You might enjoy walking your neighborhood in the evenings or going for a hike on a nearby trail in the mornings. If you enjoy being outside, you may like gardening or biking outdoors. Join a rec league kickball team, take up tennis, or shoot some hoops. You could even bust out your old rollerblades or go jump on your kid's trampoline.

Think, too, about what you can realistically do on a regular basis. Deciding you're going to take up kayaking when the closest body of water is three hours away probably won't happen during the week—though it may be nice for some Saturdays. Don't forget to set yourself up for success by hydrating, eating nutritious food, supplementing appropriately, and wearing appropriate clothes.

And always celebrate even your smallest wins. Listening to what your body needs will build your momentum and inspire you to keep it up.

Healing is a challenging journey, but it is a process that can increase your endurance, deepen your resilience, and strengthen your body. You can empower your body to tackle the challenging tasks that it can, indeed, do. Your "I did it" of today can certainly be your own inspiration to do it again tomorrow!

When a challenge presents itself—if there's something you've found difficult to master and have wanted to give up on, haven't wanted to do because it feels too hard—do it. The Word of the Lord says whatever your hand finds to do, do it with all your strength. And don't worry—God sustains you; God helps you. You are more than a conqueror.

Go and do the hard thing you need to do today. I'm rooting for you!

FULFILLING THE PURPOSE OF OUR LIVES

CHAPTER 16

WEAR "THE RIGHT SHOES"

By the end of a forty-year desert period, Israel was more structured, disciplined, and spiritually prepared—ready to enter the Promised Land. They were transformed as a whole people, as one nation. They had progressed through the desert—accepting the season (realization), deepening their dependence on God (formation), and cultivating spiritual discipline (preparation).

In this way, the healing journey parallels their journey: realizing the need for, forming an understanding of, and preparing to engage in healing—all with a focus on the Lord.

I gained wisdom about my emotional, spiritual, mental, and physical being during my own healing journey. Like the Israelites, I discovered my voice from within the desert, cried out with my voice inside the desert, and prepared my voice through the desert with the help of the Lord. Now, I aim to love God with my voice by sharing my story of healing and the Lord's great goodness in my life.

In the same way we learn from the Israelites story, I hope others are able to learn from my own, with the aim of loving God and others with our whole being. I have learned the beautiful blessing of taking care of the heart, soul, mind, and strength.

With your mind focused on things above, you will experience that same blessing—and go on to share it with others as well. And there is no greater blessing than that.

Gospel Shoes

If you've ever been to a runner's club store or a tennis-shoe-fitting store, you know it is a whole setup.

When I started running, I grabbed the only pair of tennis shoes I saw in my closet. They were five years old. Knowing what I know now, I warn strongly against wearing running shoes anywhere close to that long. Come to find out, runners are supposed to get new shoes every three-hundred to five-hundred miles. I had long since surpassed those mile markers because I'd gotten that pair before I had kids. Plus, my body changed after having both my kids. It seemed like after childbirth, my body rebuilt its bones and joints, and my muscles had shifted. (That's not the medical description, but it's certainly what it seemed like to me.) Needless to say, running had become very uncomfortable in the shoes I was wearing.

So, off I went to the runner's store for new shoes. And they go all out. They measured my gait, tracked how I moved my heels, watched where my foot lands—the whole nine yards. Turns out, I was wearing shoes that were a whole size and a half smaller than what I needed. My running shoes were way too small because my feet had actually grown after giving birth. That's why training had been so hard—I was wearing the wrong size shoes!

I got those new shoes, and I was—literally—off to the races. The first day I ran with them, I actually overran the initial distance of that day's training because my feet felt so light! I had so much energy when I started, I was startled. I was floored at how much easier running became once I got the right shoes in the right size.

This whole running-shoe-size fiasco got me thinking. We, as children of God, have spiritual armor. Paul describes the Armor of God in Ephesians 6: "Therefore put on the full armor of God, so that when the day of evil comes, you may be able to stand your ground, and after you have done everything, to stand. Stand firm then, with the belt of truth buckled around your waist, with the breastplate of righteousness in place" (vv. 13-14). Paul doesn't omit mentioning our feet. He continues, "with your feet fitted with the readiness that comes from the gospel of peace" (v. 15). Our feet are to be fitted with the *readiness* that comes from the Gospel—the Gospel that is Jesus Christ, the good news of salvation.

Many of us, in our walk with Christ, struggle and feel pain sharing or living out our faith because our "Gospel shoes" are too small. In other words, our knowledge or experience of the Gospel of Jesus Christ is limited. We haven't expanded our understanding of the Gospel—found in the Word of God. Life distracts us and takes our attention. But the Bible is clear: we must search the Scriptures, seek God more, learn more of Christ, and know the Holy Spirit more deeply so we can be better ambassadors of this Good News for the world.

We have Jesus—Christ who came, died on the cross, rose on the third day to save us and *give us abundant life*. So, how big or small are your Gospel shoes? How much priority are you giving to sharing Christ with others—not just by words but in action?

These questions stay on my mind, and I'm the first to admit—even being on stages, leading worship, and having the privilege of people seeing my work (which is all by God's grace)—sometimes my Gospel gets small. I get so busy that someone passing me in the supermarket doesn't even experience Christ through me. I love to be productive, but I have to be mindful that my productivity doesn't get in the way of loving people. After all, that's the whole point: to glorify God in all I do.

The takeaway for all of us: If your shoes are too small—get bigger ones. If your Gospel shoes are too small—expand them.

Get into the Word, meditate on what is good, honest, pure, and noble. If anything is excellent or praiseworthy—think on these things. Above all, love the Lord your God with all your heart, soul, mind, and strength. And love your neighbor by expressing love to them and for them with the Gospel.

Armoring Every Part of Our Being

We need each part of our being—heart, soul, mind, body—to be healed. Each integral part of the self needs individual care. They are important separately, and they also influence each other. They rely on each other to be able to function at their best. So, we must absolutely attend to each one with considerable care.

Your *heart* must be healed of emotional wounds. Emotions need to be balanced and regulated.

Your *soul* must be released from any stronghold not of the Spirit of God. All spiritual doors must be closed to the enemy.

Your *mind* must take captive your thoughts and submit even those in the subconscious to Jesus in obedience.

Your *strength* must come to know its full capacity to achieve what the body is capable of.

Paul concludes his description of the Armor of God saying, "Take up the shield of faith, with which you can extinguish all the flaming arrows of the evil one. Take the helmet of salvation and the sword of the Spirit, which is the word of God" (vv. 16-17). We are given spiritual resources to resist spiritual opposition and stand strong in our faith. We are called to be good stewards, owning our responsibility to heal and armoring our being for the life before us.

Healing the whole being—heart, soul, mind, and strength—is essential for living fully into the purpose for which we were created. When we are healed, we can reflect God's image and bring Him glory through our emotions, thoughts, actions, and relationships.

When we are whole, we can fulfill the purpose of life—to bring glory to God.

CHAPTER 17

WORDS OF ENCOURAGEMENT

Healing can happen at any stage in a Christian's life, and choosing to heal does not make anyone "less" Christian. Arguably, doing so makes someone a stronger one.

After leading a double life, straddling a line of living right and wrong for a couple years, and giving God a plea, He revealed himself to me in a very personal way—in the middle of a restaurant parking lot through a lady I had never seen before. She spoke to me as though she had been following me around for the past three months of my life, and I knew her prophetic words were from the Lord. Her wise counsel aligned with Scripture, glorified the Lord, and brought me peace. That August, in 2003, I dedicated my life to the Lord.

But my whole healing journey didn't begin until long after that month and year. With an unacknowledged but very present mental health disorder, I chose healing once the signs were too obvious to ignore, too crippling to continue. There's no sugarcoating the difficulty in choosing to heal because, at the same time you choose to heal, you also choose to admit you're broken. I could have kept trying to pretend everything was fine to keep up appearances and shield myself from any unwanted judgement. I could have kept going along as I had been, internalizing my struggles and avoiding them with all my might. But at what cost? I'm eternally grateful I did not keep pretending, internalizing, or avoiding.

Your struggles may not be as severe as mine were. I pray that they aren't. But ignoring mild, low-grade, or tolerable concerns can allow them to become extreme, critical, and even dire. My symptoms didn't start as severe as they eventually became, but left unhealed, they worsened over time. We all have healing to do because we are all human. Everyone's healing process is different, but everyone needs that journey. And if we do not choose to journey out of the desert, we will remain in the desert. But this does not need to be the case!

Sometimes as Christians, we take really good care of things of the spirit, but we neglect our heart, mind, and strength. When we do not love ourselves enough to take care of each part of our being, we absolutely neglect loving others. We are incapable of loving them fully, in the way Jesus instructs. The healing journey uncovered that for me.

If you want to advance in your ministry, in your walk with God, in your relationship with your family, you must ask the questions: What is the health of each of the four parts of my being? How is my heart? What's going on in my soul? Where is my mind? How is my strength? Am I really able to give of them fully?

If you aren't, that is ok—but you have to heal, to go through the process, to walk the journey of painful emotions, difficult conversations, and hard discoveries. But do it to heal so that you can become the very best of yourself to glorify the Lord in the greatest way you can.

Shame kept me from seeking the help that I needed for a long time. What are people going to think? That I get up on stages and preach life, but everything that is in me cries out death? What are people going to say about me? About the God that I preach? These thoughts weighed heavy on me, and I did everything in my power to hide how I was really feeling. But as you've learned from my journey, people expressed their encouragement to me and were encouraged by my testimony. The Lord met me in the middle of my journey and fulfilled His promise to give abundant life. And the God I preach? He gave me strength, courage, and freedom through His son Jesus.

God will go with you on your healing journey—he promises us that. When you ask Him to be with you, He will be. God's presence mattered so much to Moses that he said to God, "If your Presence does not go with us, do not send us up from here" (Exodus 33:15). Moses and the Israelites came to realize that entering the Promised Land without God would be meaningless. He continued, asking, "What else will distinguish me and your people from all the other people on the face of the earth?" (v. 16). They had come to see that land itself was not the ultimate promise—God's nearness was. The Israelites learned that it was God's presence that gave them their identity, meaning, and purpose.

God will be near to you on your healing journey—through stages of realization, formation, preparation, and transformation. As you discover your voice from within the desert, cry out with your voice inside the desert, and prepare your voice through the desert, He will be with you. And once you are out of the desert, you will be able to love God with your voice—fully, with your whole being. God helped me on my healing journey, and He will continue to help me each day—just as He will with you.

You will make your way out of the desert, and your desert season will come to an end. But keep in mind that healing never really ends. Once your being is whole, healing becomes maintenance work, but we must keep at it—constantly healing, constantly focused on the Lord. For the Word also says: "If you think you are standing strong, be careful not to fall" (1 Corinthians 10:12, NLT).

Today, right now in this moment, I invite you to choose healing. No matter where you find yourself—no matter your season or distance inside a desert—your healing can begin today. Let these words be an invitation to step forward in hope, trusting that restoration is always possible.

In this life, we will have trouble. But we can take heart—because Jesus has overcome the world and given us freedom and abundant life in him!

What good, Good News. There is none better for our heart, soul, mind, and strength.

AFTERWORD

THE TREASURE AT THE END OF THE DESERT

When I began this journey, I thought I was setting out to win a war.

A war with my mind, with the heaviness in my chest, with the shadows that seemed to stretch further than any sunrise could ever reach. And I fought—hard. Every day felt like a battlefield of thoughts, emotions, and memories—welcomed and not. My soul's bloody knuckles clawed through the wilderness of my mind, thirsty for something I couldn't name.

But the desert has a way of teaching you what really matters.

What I found, buried under all the after-storm sands, was not a quick answer, not a magic cure, but a truth older than the ground I walked on. It was the *Shema*—the premise of our lives. And that day it became the premise of mine:

> *Hear, O Israel: The Lord your God, the Lord is ONE. And you shall love the Lord your God with all your heart, with all your soul, with all your mind, and with all your strength. And love your neighbor as yourself.*

God is One. Father, the Son, and Holy Spirit—perfect unity, balance, harmony. And I am called, as His child, to mirror that unity—to bring heart, mind, soul, and strength together as one, just as my Creator made me to. From there, love would overflow—a love so pure it aches, like his heart for His children, His children. Overcoming suffering cleared the fogged lenses of my life, and I could see Love. I could see Him.

I thought healing would be the end of the story. But healing was the only road. The road that led me to love—not the fragile, rationed kind we protect with walls and conditions, but eternal, unbreakable love that begins in God and moves through us like breath.

That love is the true treasure.

Love is not just an emotion—it's a substance from the eternal realm, placed in us for this temporary life. The only thing we carry from here into eternity. Every forgiveness, every unseen kindness, every time you chose mercy over judgement—all of it will stand with you, whole and unbroken, in the presence of the One who is Love.

And God does not lose what belongs to Him

This is why the enemy fights love harder than anything else. He can counterfeit miracles, manipulate power, mimic beauty and wisdom, twist truth, and even dress up false holiness. But he cannot create love. That requires God's nature living within someone. His only tactic is to scare you out of giving it. But love—real love—is God's most unstoppable weapon. It's the "nuclear" force of the Kingdom. The very thing that breaks fear's grip and silences the accuser.

Revelation tells us we overcome "by the blood of the Lamb, by the word of our testimony, and because we did not love our lives so much as to shrink from death"(12:11). That last part—loving God and others more than we love our own comfort or safety—is the kind of love the enemy has no defense against.

The blood secures the covenant.
The testimony makes it known.
And Love—fierce, stubborn, self-giving love—breaks the back of fear.

This Love paired with a full abiding in God is all we truly need. He does the rest.

This was the treasure I found in the desert.

And now I know it's the treasure we were created to live in all along:

To *love God* with everything we are.

To *love others* with the same grace that rescued us.

To *live with love* that will still be here when the battles are over and the dust has settled.

Because love is not what survives the fight. Love walks you right on through the desert and back home. Love is not a pause in battle—it's the voice that fuels the battle cry that leads from brokenness to freedom.

Love doesn't lead you to the win—love *is* the victory.